HYMNS

of

Praise, Prayer, and Devout Meditation.

BY JOSIAH CONDER.

Prepared for Publication by the Author.

LONDON:
JOHN SNOW, PATERNOSTER ROW.
MDCCCLVI.

Preface.

These Hymns are the echoes of a harp but just silenced on earth, and newly tuned and strung to the harmonies of heaven. The preparation of the volume had occupied much of its Author's time and thought during the closing year of his life, and he had revised for the press all but the last two or three sheets, when the arresting hand of Death was gently laid upon him, and he was called, sooner than he or those around him anticipated, but not sooner than was timeliest and wisest, to rest from all earthly labour, and to enter into the joy of his Lord. Could he have foreseen it, there is, probably, no other work which he would have so well liked to be his latest earthly employment, and his memorial among those by whom he most wished to be remembered, as there is scarcely any other which could seem so happily fitted to prepare the spirit for the awful though blissful transition from the din, and strife, and toil of political and ecclesiastical controversy, and the imperfect and broken fellowship of the church militant, to the pure and peaceful communion of the 'spirits of the just made perfect,' in the presence of their Lord and ours.

The volume might have been intituled "The Hymns of a Life-time," for the dates of its various compositions reach from the threshold of manhood to the precincts of old age. Several of them were written more than forty years ago, and were published, in the year 1824, in a volume intituled "*The Star in the East, and other Poems.*" The most popular of these early compositions—possibly, of all the productions of the writer's pen, the one which has made his name the most widely known and loved amongst Christians of very different sections of the Universal Church, had been previously published (A. D. 1812) in the second edition of "*The Associate Minstrels,*" the joint work of several kindred spirits. Through the changing experiences and incessant toils of a long and busy life, sacred song continued to be the refreshment and solace of a mind whose favourite pursuits were religious, and whose most welcome recreation was change of activity. In the year 1837, the Author published a second volume of poems, under the title of "*The Choir and the Oratory, or Praise and Prayer*," in which many of the Hymns of the present volume were included. Others were published in the *Congregational Hymn Book*, some of them having been composed while that work was in progress, in order to supply felt deficiencies. A considerable portion, the fruit of later years, are now published for the first time.

The first section of the volume consists of versions of Psalms, for the most part singularly close. These by no means include all the Psalms rendered into verse by the Author, who took especial delight in the study of that portion of inspired Scripture, but those only which he deemed capable of being treated as 'Hymns;' *i. e.*, lyrical compositions suited for Christian worship, whether social or solitary. The other sections into which the Hymns are classed will need no explanation. The "Hymns of Praise" furnish a beautiful memorial of the Author's devout spirit; and the

"Collects in Verse," (as coming from the pen of so staunch a Nonconformist) of his catholic sympathy with true piety, wherever met with. Of the "Hymns founded on Passages of Scripture," many were suggested by particular discourses, either heard or preached; some were night thoughts, when poetry and devout musing supplied the refreshment which sleep denied. With reference to several of the Hymns in this section of the book, the Writer repeatedly observed that he did not regard them as possessing much poetical merit, but that they contained important and sometimes neglected scriptural ideas, which had been profitable and impressive to his own mind, and might prove so to others. He was content, in these instances, that but little admiration should be awarded to the vehicle in which the thought was presented, provided that it served its purpose.

Many of the Hymns are transcripts of personal experience, and add to the proofs so often given, that God tunes the heart by trial and sorrow, not only to patience but to praise. Not a few have been composed during the last two years of their

Author's earthly life; a period marked off from the rest by the heavy shadows of domestic sorrow, but not the less devoted, with untiring faithfulness, to the service of the church and of his country, and brightened by the retrospect of so many years of mercy, and still more by the unclouded prospect of that eternal rest into which he has now entered.

It was matter of regret with the Author, when it became evident that he would probably never be permitted to resume the pen, that he had not written a Preface to this edition of his collected Hymns. He had intended to give some explanations, the exact nature of which it is impossible to ascertain; his extreme weakness during the last three weeks of his illness having disabled him for prolonged conversation. It is hoped, however, that the substance of much that he would have said is conveyed in the foregoing remarks. It will be interesting to the friends of the departed poet to know, that the contents of this little volume, the composition of which had so often been the solace of his active life, helped to soothe and cheer him, as his path entered the Valley of the Shadow. "His Hymns," he said, "while they reproved him, comforted him." He desired to have those read to him which spoke of the Lord Jesus. A few evenings before his departure, those commencing, "They whom the Father giveth" (p. 165), and "Upholden by the hand" (p. 166), were read to him at his own request. Of the latter, he said that he had composed it "as a death-bed hymn." As he found a difficulty in fixing his attention, it was read three times, and he then said he had it by heart. "Now you can sleep upon that," said one of his children. "Oh, yes," was the emphatic answer, "and *die* upon it."

It may be interesting to add, that the Hymn at page 169, (published in the first editions of the Congregational Hymn Book, but afterwards omitted,) was written with a view of furnishing words expressive of Christian faith and feeling to the music adapted to Pope's popular ode, "Vital spark," which has nothing distinctively Christian about it but the title. Also, that the Hymn at page 121 ("Day ever blessed") was written to a very sweet air in the "*Chants Chrétiens*," set to the words "Jour du Seigneur," &c.

Although the last two sheets have been sent to press since the removal of their Author, their contents, including the Hymns by Mrs. JOSIAH CONDER, had been prepared and arranged for publication by himself. One addition only has been ventured on. During the last year or two he had taken considerable interest in rendering some of his own hymns into Latin, upon the model, not of the classic measures, but of the mediæval Latin hymns, many of which are alike simple, terse, and beautiful. One specimen of these—a version of the hymn commencing, " Thou art the Everlasting Word"—has been appended at the close of the volume.

This collected edition of the hymns of JOSIAH CONDER is now sent forth by those to whom he bequeathed this sacred task, in the earnest hope that, while to his personal friends it will be a most valued and appropriate memorial of him who, for a little time, is parted from us,—" not lost, but gone before,"—it will help to nourish the piety, soothe the sorrows, and animate the courage of many a fellow-pilgrim to whom he was personally unknown, and to minister to the edification of the Holy Catholic Church of Christ, comprehending all true Christians of every name, the prosperity and unity of which formed one of the dearest wishes of his heart.

E. R.C.

St. John's Wood,
      January, 1856.

TABLE OF CONTENTS.

Versions of Psalms.

	PAGE
Why do the heathen rage?	1
To Thee, my righteous Judge, to Thee	2
How long wilt thou forget me	3
Thee will I love, O God, and own	4
The Heavens declare His glory	5
In the day of thy distress	7
The Lord my shepherd is	8
The Lord is my shepherd, and I am His sheep	10
For ever will I bless the Lord	11
As high as the heavens, and as vast	13
God is our refuge ever near	14
Truly I on God depend	15
Praise on Thee, in Zion-gates	16
Be merciful, O God of grace	17
How honoured, how dear	18
Oh, sing unto Jehovah a new song	21
Earth, rejoice! Jehovah reigns	23
O sing to the Lord a new song	24
Oh, be joyful in the Lord	26
Praise the Lord. With all my heart	27
Hallelujah. Raise, Oh raise	29
Jehovah's praise sublime	30

	PAGE
Thy hands have made and fashioned me	31
Lord! how I love Thy law	32
Out of the deep I sighed	33
Hope, ye mourners, in the Lord	34
To our God loud praises give	35
I will extol Thy name, O God, my king	36

Hymns of Praise and Adoration.

To Him who is above all height	41
Now with angels round the throne	43
Creator of all being	44
Heavenly Father! all things came	45
Father of Spirits! God of heaven!	46
Holy, holy, holy Lord	47
Father of eternal grace	48
Oh, give thanks to Him who made	49
'Tis good, in tuneful verses	50
Praise the God of all creation	51
Lord God, our heavenly Father, be	52
Beyond, beyond that boundless sea	53
O Thou who givest all their food	55
O Thou, whose covenant is sure	56
Oh, love beyond the reach of thought	57
Thou art the everlasting Word	59
Substantial truth, O Christ, thou art	61
Lamb of God, who didst sustain	63
Wheresoever two or three	64
Grant me, heavenly Lord! to feel	65
Come, Lord Jesus! haste the day	66
O Thou, our Head, enthroned on high	68
Head of the Church, our risen Lord	69

	PAGE
Oh, breathe upon this languid frame	70
Leave us not comfortless	71
O God, from whom is my desire	72
My Lord! I recognize Thy claim	73
I am Thy workmanship, O Lord!	74
Lord! whate'er in mortal eyes	76
O thou God, who hearest prayer	77
Yes, my God, Thy will is best	78
Oh, for the spirit of a child	79
How shall I follow Him I serve?	80
When in the hour of lonely woe	82
'Tis not that I did choose Thee	84
Far from my thoughts, vain world, depart	85
Bread of Heaven! on Thee I feed	86
O thou Divine High Priest	87
O God, who didst Thy will unfold	88
Lord, for Thy name's sake! Such the plea	90
O God! who didst an equal mate	91
The peace of God, transcending	92

Collects in Verse.

O God, whose blessed Son as man appeared	95
O God, who didst for man's salvation	96
Eternal God, who hatest	96
Baptized into our Saviour's death	97
Thou knowest, Lord, on every hand	97
O God, whose sovereign power and skill	98
O God, who art the strength of all	99
O God, protector of the lowly	99
Grant, O Saviour, to our prayers	100
O God, who hast such bliss prepared	100
Lord of all power and might	101

CONTENTS.

	PAGE
O God, whose never-failing providence	101
O God, who dost Thy sovereign might	102
Eternal Father, God of Peace!	102
Since, gracious God! apart from Thee	103
To all Thy faithful people, Lord	103
O God, from whom all that is good proceeds	104
O God, to whom our hearts lie all revealed	104
With Thy most gracious favour, Lord	105
Almighty God, who on the Eternal Rock	105
O God, whose grace has knit in one communion	106
O God, to whom the happy dead	106

Hymns founded on Passages of Holy Scripture.

Thy voice, O Lord! I hear not	109
Not Thy permission, Lord, I ask	111
O Lord! I ask not for the sight	112
Exile who, on foreign strand	113
Oh, say not, think not in thy heart	114
If the Lord had felt displeasure	115
God's good time with patience wait	116
When, courting slumber	117
Angels, ye who ne'er can know	118
Churches of Christ, by God's right-hand	120
Day ever blessed	121
Blessed be God! He is not strict	123
Now is born the promised child	124
Upon a world of guilt and night	125
The Cross, the Cross on which He died	126
Oh, shew me not my Saviour dying	128
Christ our Lord arose to-day	130
To His own world He came	131
Oh, mystery transcending thought	133

CONTENTS.

	PAGE
Art thou a scholar of the word?	135
Day by day the manna fell	137
Father! to Thy sinful child	138
Heavenly Father, to whose eye	140
Oh, comfort to the dreary	142
Transporting thought! The Master's joy	144
Oh, how shall feeble flesh and blood	146
As much have I of worldly good	147
Long have I toiled with hope deferred	148
That Name of power! which Satan heard	149
My wealth is in a world of joy	151
Welcome, welcome! Sinner, hear!	152
Son of David, throned in light	154
They whom the Father giveth	155
O Lord! hadst Thou been here! But when	158
Whither, when I drop this clay	159
How safe were those whom Jesus kept	160
No condemnation, no condemnation	161
How sweet, from crowded throngs	162
If all the world abhor us	164
When I can trust my all with God	165
Upholden by the hand	166
Eighteen centuries have fled	167
If the dead rise not, then is Christ not raised	168
Vital spark of heavenly flame	169
Lord! does Thy word of promise say	170
Followers of Christ, of every name	171
I will take refuge in my God	173
Sons of God, while here below	174
Lord Christ, our glorious Head! in Thee	175
What mean the sophists cold	176
Yet, canst thou pray indeed	178
Yet, deem not prayer in vain	180
Oh, how should those be clean who bear	182
What joy, when life seems almost spent	183
Forerunner of His ransomed Host	184

CONTENTS.

	PAGE
Come to the House of Prayer	185
Comrades of the heavenly calling	186
What if those registered on high	188
We have an Altar, not of stone	189
When anxious thoughts the bosom fill	190
Art thou discipled to the Lord	191
Oh, the hour when this material	192
The followers of the Lamb who stand	195
The Lord is King! lift up thy voice	196
Already dawns that glorious day	198
See the ransomed millions stand	200
Shepherd of thine Israel! lead us	201
DIVINE FOOTPRINTS	202

Hymns by Mrs. Josiah Conder.

Their Lord was sleeping on a pillow	207
Not Thy garment's hem alone	209
When Mary to the Heavenly Guest	210
Sad night and blissful morn	212
The hours of evening close	214
Land of the free indeed	215
What blissful harmonies above	216

AGNUS DEI	218

VERSIONS OF PSALMS.

VERSIONS OF PSALMS.

"Why do the heathen rage?"—Psalm ii.

WHY do the heathen rage,
    Despot and priest conspire?
Why, rebels, with your God engage,
    And tempt Jehovah's ire?

    Messiah, promised long,
      Yet, scorned and crucified,
Now, amid Heaven's adoring throng,
    Reigns at the Father's side.

    The day on which He rose,
      Proclaimed Him Son of God.
His grace has triumphed o'er His foes:
    Oh, kiss His kingly rod.

    We own Thy rightful claim:
      We bow before Thy throne.
Let sinners learn Thy saving name,
    And trust in Thee alone.

PSALM IV.

"Hear me when I call, O God of my righteousness."—Psalm iv.

TO Thee, my righteous Judge, to Thee,
My Justifier, Lord, I flee:
On Thee, my aid in troubles past,
Again my fainting soul I cast.

How long will ye, O sons of pride,
My claims contemn, my hopes deride?
How long pursue your impious schemes,
Trusting in fictions, courting dreams?

Know that the God in whom I trust,
Regards with favouring eye the just:
His chosen ones He makes His care,
And He will hearken to my prayer.

Then, tremble to oppose His will;
Commune with conscience and be still:
With righteous hands your offerings bring,
And put your trust in Israel's King.

The worldling's search for bliss is vain:
Lord! let me but Thy favour gain:
A purer joy Thy smile affords,
Than plenteous crops or golden hoards.

PSALM XIII.

So will I lay me down and sleep
In peace, for Thou my rest wilt keep.
Thou art my trust, my sure defence;
My shield is Thine Omnipotence.

" How long wilt Thou forget me?"—Psalm xiii.

How long wilt Thou forget me,
  O Lord? For evermore?
For ever wilt Thou let me
  Thine absent face deplore?
Oh! do not Thou forsake me:
  Dispel this heavy gloom,
Lest fatal sleep o'ertake me,
  The death-sleep of the tomb.

Lord! in my tribulation,
  I trust Thy mercy still;
And surely Thy salvation
  My heart with joy shall fill.
Thine aid Thou didst afford me;
  Thy praises I will sing;
And, for His mercy toward me,
  I bless my God and King.

"I will love Thee, O Lord, my strength."—Psalm xviii.

THEE will I love, O God, and own,
My strength is in Thine arm alone.
Jehovah is my rock, my tower,
My Saviour in the darkest hour;
My God, my strength, my confidence,
My buckler, helm, and high defence.
On Him I call, and bless His name:
Ne'er shall my hope be put to shame.

With forms of death on every side,
Beset with foes, my courage died:
Hell compassed me with horrors dread;
The snares of death were round me spread:
In my distress to God I prayed;
I called upon my God for aid:
He heard my cry; it reached His throne.
Thee will I love, O God, alone.

PSALM XIX.

"The heavens declare the glory of God."—Psalm xix.

THE HEAVENS declare His glory,
   Their Maker's skill the skies:
Each day repeats the story,
   And night to night replies.
Their silent proclamation
   Throughout the earth is heard;
The record of Creation,
   The page of Nature's word.

There, from His bright pavilion,
   Like eastern bridegroom clad,
Hailed by earth's thousand million,
   The sun sets forth: right glad,
His glorious race commencing,
   The mighty giant seems;
Through the vast round dispensing
   His all-pervading beams.

So pure, so soul-restoring,
   Is Truth's diviner ray;
A brighter radiance pouring
   Than all the pomp of day:
The wanderer surely guiding,
   It makes the simple wise;
And, evermore abiding,
   Unfailing joy supplies.

PSALM XIX.

Thy word is richer treasure
  Than lurks within the mine;
And daintiest fare less pleasure
  Yields, than this food divine.
How wise each kind monition!
  Led by Thy counsels, Lord,
How safe the saints' condition,
  How great is their reward!

But past transgressions pain me:
  Lord! cleanse my heart within;
And evermore restrain me
  From all presumptuous sin.
So let my whole behaviour,
  Thoughts, words, and actions, be,
O God, my Strength and Saviour,
  Acceptable to Thee.

PSALM XX.

"The Lord hear thee in the day of trouble!" —Psalm xx.

IN the day of thy distress,
   May Jehovah hear thee!
In the hour when dangers press,
   Jacob's God be near thee:
Send thee, from His holy place,
Timely aid or strengthening grace!

May thy prayers and offerings rise,
   By thy God recorded!
Thine oblations reach the skies,
   Graciously rewarded!
Granted be thy heart's request;
All thy purposes be blest!

Thy success our hearts shall cheer:
   We, with exultation,
In Jehovah's name will rear
   Trophies of salvation.
Go beneath His guardian care,
And The Lord fulfil thy prayer!

Vain the despot's haughty boasts,
   Fleets or martial forces:
Be our trust the God of Hosts,
   Heavenly our resources.
Theirs shall be defeat and shame:
We shall triumph in Thy name.

PSALM XXIII.

"The Lord is my Shepherd: I shall not want."—Psalm xxiii.

THE LORD my Shepherd is,
    And He my soul will keep:
He knoweth who are His,
    And watcheth o'er His sheep.
Away with every anxious fear:
I cannot want while He is near.

His wisdom doth provide
    The pasture where I feed:
Where the still waters glide
    Along the quiet mead,
He leads my feet; and, when I roam,
O'ertakes and brings the wanderer home.

He leads, Himself, the way
    His faithful flock should take.
Them who His voice obey,
    His love will ne'er forsake:
For He has pledged His holy name;—
He who for ever is the same.

PSALM XXIII.

Let me but feel Him near,
   Death's gloomy pass in view,
I'll walk without a fear
   The shadowy valley through.
With rod and staff, my Shepherd's care
Will guide my steps, and guard me there.

Still is my table spread;
   My foes stand silent by.
I feed on living bread;
   My cruse is never dry:
And surely love and mercy will
Attend me on my journey still.

Still hope and grateful praise
   Shall form my constant song;
Shall cheer my gloomiest days,
   And tune my dying tongue:
Until my ransomed soul shall rise,
To praise Him better in the skies.

ANOTHER VERSION.

"The Lord is my Shepherd: I shall not want."—Psalm xxiii.

THE LORD is my Shepherd, and I am His sheep:
From want and from danger His flock He will keep.
In pastures all verdant by night I abide,
And He chooses my path where the cool waters glide.

If ever I wander, as silly sheep roam,
He seeks His poor truant and leads me safe home;
Then shows by His footsteps the way I should take,
And, true to His promise, will never forsake.

When, gloomy my path, the deep valleys I tread,
All darkness before from the rocks overhead,
My Shepherd is with me, why fear any ill?
His crook and His staff they shall comfort me still.

My enemies frown, but they can do no more:
My wants are supplied till my cup runneth o'er.
Surely goodness and mercy my days shall attend,
Till I reach the bright mansions of joy without end.

PSALM XXXIV.

" I will bless the Lord at all times."—Psalm xxxiv.

FOR ever will I bless The Lord,
   Nor cease His praise to speak :
My song His goodness shall record,
   That the oppressed and weak
May trust in Him, who will reward
   The humble and the meek.

Oh, magnify The Lord with me !
   Come, join His name to bless :
To Him did I in trouble flee ;
   He saved me from distress.
Oh, let Him, then, your refuge be,
   Nor shall you fail success.

He is a God who heareth prayer :
   He raised me from the dust.
His angel-bands keep station where
   Dangers would harm the just.
Then, try His love, and trust His care :
   Blessed are they who trust.

Oh, fear The Lord, ye saints of His ;
   Make Him your trust and dread :
Then cast off every care but this ;
   For He will give you bread.
The famished beast its prey may miss ;
   His children shall be fed.

PSALM XXXIV.

Ye who would length of days attain,
   And have your joy increase,
Let truth your guarded lips restrain;
   From guile and falsehood cease;
From malice and revenge refrain,
   And follow after peace.

God on His saints looks watchful down;
   His ear attends their cry.
The wicked sink beneath His frown;
   Their very name shall die:
But He at length the just will crown
   With joy and victory.

The broken heart His grace shall heal;
   His hand the contrite raise.
Many the woes the righteous feel;
   Yet still, in all their ways,
Kept by His power, they bear the seal
   Of His redeeming grace.

Evil shall be its own reward,
   And just the sinner's fate;
But Thou our ransom didst afford:
   Thy mercy, Lord, we wait:
And none who wait upon The Lord,
   Shall e'er be desolate.

PSALM XXXVI.

"Thy mercy, O Lord, is in the heavens."—Psalm xxxvi.

AS high as the heavens, and as vast,
   Thy mercy, O God, has no bound!
Thy laws like the mountains stand fast;
   Thy judgments no plummet can sound.

All creatures Thy providence share:
   Thy bounty, how sovereign and free!
To Thee, as the Hearer of prayer,
   All mortals for refuge may flee.

The poor in Thy house are supplied,
   Where freely Thy gifts are bestowed;
And they drink the pure waters that glide
   Through the courts of Thy hallowed abode.

With Thee is the fountain of life:
   Lord! grant us to drink of that spring;
And o'er the world's sorrow and strife
   The light of Thy promises fling.

Continue Thy love to Thy saints;
   To the just Thy protection extend;
On the wicked impose Thy restraints,
   And the weak from oppression defend.

PSALM XLVI.

"God is our refuge and strength."—Psalm xlvi. 1-5.

GOD is our refuge ever near,
   Our help in tribulation:
Therefore His people shall not fear
   Amid a wrecked creation.
Though mountains from their base be hurled,
And ocean shake the solid world,
   The Lord is our salvation.

The stream that flows from Sion's hill,
   Shall yet, serenely gliding,
With joy the holy city fill,
   His presence there abiding.
The Lord, her glory and defence,
Will guard His chosen residence,
   His timely aid providing.

PSALM LXII.

"Truly my soul waiteth upon God: from Him cometh my salvation."—Psalm lxii.

TRULY I on God depend,
   God, my Saviour and my Friend.
His protection is my tower,
My retreat in danger's hour.

Wait, my soul, on Him alone;
Wait for succour from His throne:
Friends may fail, the world may frown;
I shall never be cast down.

Trust in Him for evermore:
Ye, His people, freely pour
In His ear your sad complaints,
Strength and Refuge of His saints.

Treacherous are the fickle crowd,
False the noble and the proud:
Trust not to unrighteous gain,
Fleeting wealth and honour vain.

More than once hath God made known,
Power belongs to Him alone:
Mercy, too, belongs to Thee;
Mercy joined with equity.

PSALM LXV.

"Praise waiteth for Thee, O God, in Zion."—Psalm lxv.

PRAISE on Thee, in Zion-gates,
   Daily, O Jehovah! waits:
Unto Thee who hearest prayer,
Shall the tribes of men repair.

Though with conscious guilt oppressed,
On Thy mercy still we rest:
Thy forgiving love display;
Take, O Lord, our sins away.

Oh, how blessed their reward,
Chosen servants of The Lord,
Who within Thy courts abide,
With Thy goodness satisfied!

But how dire Thy judgments fell,
Saviour of Thine Israel,
When Thy people's cry arose,
On their proud and impious foes!

By Thy boundless might set fast,
Rise the mountains firm and vast:
Thou canst with a word assuage
Ocean's wild and deafening rage.

When Thy signs in heaven appear,
Earth's remotest regions fear;
And the bounties of Thy hand
Fill with gladness every land.

PSALM LXVII.

"God be merciful unto us and bless us."—Psalm lxvii.

BE merciful, O God of grace!
  Show us the brightness of Thy face;
That Thy redeemed Church may shine,
In this dark world, with light divine.

That light divine, oh, let it spread,
Till all the darkness shall have fled;
And the false crescent's fading ray
Be lost in the full noon of day.

Reveal, O Lord, Thy saving plan
To all the families of man:
Let distant nations hear Thy word;
Let every people praise The Lord.

Let them with joy Thy praises sing,
Earth's righteous Judge and sovereign King:
Illumined by Thy holy word,
Let all the nations praise The Lord.

Then shall this barren world assume
New beauty, and the desert bloom:
Our God shall richly bless us then;
And all men fear His name.   Amen.

PSALM LXXXIV.

"How amiable are Thy tabernacles."—Psalm lxxxiv.

HOW honoured, how dear,
   That sacred abode,
Where Christians draw near
   Their Father and God!
'Mid worldly commotion,
   My wearied soul faints
For the house of devotion,
   The home of Thy saints.

The birds have their home;
   They fix on their nest:
Wherever they roam,
   They return to their rest:
From them fondly learning,
   My soul would take wing;
To Thee so returning,
   My God and my King.

Oh, happy the choirs
   Who praise Thee above!
What joy tunes their lyres!
   Their worship is love.

Yet, safe in Thy keeping,
  And happy they be,
In this world of weeping,
  Whose strength is in Thee.

Though rugged their way,
  They drink as they go,
Of springs that convey
  New life as they flow:
The God they rely on,
  Their strength shall renew,
Till each, brought to Zion,
  His glory shall view.

Thou Hearer of prayer!
  Still grant me a place,
Where Christians repair
  To the courts of Thy grace.
More blessed beyond measure
  One day so employed,
Than years of vain pleasure
  By worldlings enjoyed.

Me more would it please
  Keeping post at Thy gate,
Than lying at ease
  In chambers of state:

The meanest condition
 Outshines, with Thy smiles,
The pomp of ambition,
 The world with its wiles.

The Lord is a sun!
 The Lord is a shield!
What grace has begun,
 With glory is sealed.
He hears the distressèd;
 He succours the just;
And they shall be blessèd
 Who make Him their trust.

PSALM XCVI.

"O sing unto the Lord a new song."—Psalm xcvi.

O SING unto Jehovah a new song;
   Sing to our God, all nations of the earth:
Sing to Jehovah; His glad praise prolong;
   From day to day proclaim His glorious worth.

His glory to the Pagan world proclaim;
   Let Asia hear, and from her idols turn:
Let fettered Afric hail Jehovah's name,
   And the New World His ancient worship learn.

Great is The Lord, and greatly to be praised,
   The God of gods: Him only will we fear.
Vain idols are all other gods: He raised
   The heavens, and bade the universe appear.

Infinite Power and Majesty sublime
   Attend His steps: He dwells in glorious light.
Ascribe to Him, ye tribes of every clime,
   To Him alone, glory, and rule, and might.

O give to God the thanks that are His due;
   With offerings meet do homage at His throne.
Come, worship Him with hearts devout and true.
   Tremble, O Earth! thy Maker's presence own.

Proclaim to Nature's utmost bounds, He reigns,
   Lord God Omnipotent. Soon, soon shall cease
The world's commotions, while alone remains
   That kingdom which is righteousness and peace.

Be glad, O heavens! and let all earth rejoice;
   Ocean with all his waves exult; the dumb
Break silence, and mute Nature find a voice;
   Green fields and woods rejoice: The Lord will
     come!

He comes to judge the earth, to vindicate
   His justice and His truth; to break the chain
Of Nature's bondage,—comes to renovate
   Creation, and for evermore to reign.

"The Lord reigneth: let the earth rejoice."—Psalm xcvii.

Earth, rejoice! Jehovah reigns:
Join, ye isles, in joyful strains.
Darkness His dread seat enfolds;
Righteousness His throne upholds.

His just rule the heavens proclaim:
Thunders spoke His awful name,
When the people of His choice
Saw His glory, heard His voice.

Shame and woe shall light on all
Who on sculptured idols call.
All ye gods and heavenly powers,
Worship Him, your Lord and ours.

Lord! to earth's remotest ends,
Over all Thy rule extends:
Far above—supreme, alone,—
Every princedom, power, or throne.

Ye who love Jehovah's name,
Hate all deeds and thoughts of shame:
He preserves His saints, and will
Rescue them from every ill.

Light is for the righteous sown ;
Gladness for the just alone.
Saints, your God for ever bless ;
Triumph in His holiness.

"O sing unto the Lord a new song."—Psalm xcviii.

O SING to the Lord a new song,
   For marvellous things hath He wrought:
To Him your glad praises belong,
   Whose right arm the triumph has brought.

His people salvation have found,
   For Jehovah Himself was their aid ;
In the sight of the heathen around,
   The Lord hath His judgments displayed.

He remembered His mercy, nor turned
   From the word that to Israel He gave ;
And the ends of the earth will have learned,
   He only is able to save.

To Him let the earth raise her voice,
   All nations unite in the song ;
In accents of triumph rejoice,
   And still the loud anthem prolong.

With the harp and the music of verse,
   With trumpets in jubilant strains,
The praise of Jehovah rehearse :
   Rejoice, The Omnipotent reigns.

Let Ocean respond with his roar,
   All his waves in the chorus employ :
Let it spread through the world, shore to shore
   Repeating and spreading the joy.

From the floods, let the hills catch the strain,
   Earth's Saviour and King to adore.
He cometh, in justice to reign,
   And His throne shall endure evermore.

"Make a joyful noise unto the Lord, all ye lands."—Psalm c.

OH, be joyful in the Lord,
   Every land beneath the sun:
In His praise, with glad accord,
   Let all tongues and hearts be one.
For our God is God alone,
Whose we are, and not our own:
We His people are, the sheep
He vouchsafes to rule and keep.

Come and join the joyous throng
   Who Jehovah's praise proclaim:
In His courts, with grateful song,
   Speak the honours of His name.
Rich His bounty to our race;
Inexhaustible His grace;
Ready to forgive and bless;
Ever sure His faithfulness.

PSALM CXI.

"Praise ye the Lord. I will praise the Lord with my whole heart."—Psalm cxi.

PRAISE The Lord. With all my heart,
I will in His praise take part,
Wheresoe'er, in concord sweet,
Saints unite or churches meet.

What delight, with awe explored,
All His marvellous works afford!
Glorious are His acts of might;
His decrees supremely right.

He has caused to be enrolled,
Wonders which He wrought of old,
That remembrance of the past
Through remotest times might last.

Gracious is The Lord, and kind;
To compassion still inclined:
He supplies His people's want,
Mindful of His covenant.

He displayed in Israel's sight
All the terrors of His might;
That on them He might bestow
Kingdoms of the heathen foe.

Just the judgments of His hands;
Fixed is all that He commands:
Firm His purposes endure,
True and faithful, just and sure.

He redeemed His chosen race;
And His covenant of grace
Stands eternally the same:
Hallowed be His awful name.

Fear of God is wisdom's prime:
This is knowledge most sublime,
Which adores Him and obeys:
Everlasting is His praise.

"He raiseth the poor out of the dust."—Psalm cxiii.

HALLELUJAH. Raise, Oh raise
To our God the song of praise:
All His servants, join to sing
God our Saviour and our King.

Blessed be for evermore
That dread Name which we adore!
Round the world His praise be sung,
Through all lands, in every tongue.

O'er all nations God alone,
Higher than the heavens His throne:
Who is like to God Most High,
Infinite in majesty?

Yet, to view the heavens He bends;
Yea, to earth He condescends;
Passing by the rich and great,
For the low and desolate.

He can raise the poor to stand
With the princes of the land;
Wealth upon the needy shower,
Set the meanest high in power.

PSALM CXVII.

He the broken spirit cheers;
Turns to joy the mourner's tears:
Such the wonders of His ways!
Praise His name;—for ever praise.

"O praise the Lord, all ye nations."—Psalm cxvii.

JEHOVAH'S praise sublime
   Through the wide earth be sung:
Ye realms of every clime,
   Ye tribes of every tongue,
His infinite compassion bless,
His ever-during faithfulness.

"Thy hands have made me, and fashioned me."—Psalm cxix.
73, 64, 68, 17, 125, 171, 172.

THY hands have made and fashioned me:
I hold my being, Lord, from Thee.
Oh, teach Thy creature to fulfil
The law and purpose of Thy will.

Thy goodness clothes and fills the earth:
Each moment gives new mercies birth.
Thy richest gift, Thy grace, bestow,
And let my soul Thy mercy know.

Lord! Thou art good, and doest good;
Giver of life, and health, and food.
Teach me Thy statutes, and impart
A wise and understanding heart.

In mercy with Thy servant deal:
Thy statutes and Thy grace reveal.
I am Thy servant: by that name,
To know Thy blessed will I claim.

So shall my lips shew forth Thy praise,
When Thou hast taught me all Thy ways.
Others shall learn Thy name to bless,
For Thy commands are righteousness.

PSALM CXIX.

"Oh, how love I Thy law!"—Psalm cxix. 97, 87, 103, 72, 127, 33.

LORD! how I love Thy law,
  The transcript of Thy will;
While from Thy grace the strength I draw
  Its precepts to fulfil.

Oh, how I love Thy law,
  In all its terrors dressed,
Beholding there, with filial awe,
  A Father's will expressed.

Its curse no more I fear:
  Its threats are mercy now:
Its thunders undismayed I hear,
  Yet, all its claims allow.

No arbitrary code,
  No grievous yoke is Thine:
Though terrors fence the narrow road,
  It blooms with joys divine.

Oh, turn away mine eyes
  From forms of vain deceit:
Instruct me where my danger lies,
  And speed my loitering feet.

The sweetness of Thy word
  Excels the bee's rich store:
Thy counsels has my heart preferred
  To mines of golden ore.

Teach me to do Thy will,
  And all Thy truth impart;
Thy better covenant fulfil,
  And write it on my heart.

"Out of the depths have I cried unto Thee."—Psalm cxxx.

OUT of the deep I sighed:
  Hear me, O God, I cried;
Bend down a gracious ear.

To Thee I make confession.
Lord! shouldst Thou mark transgression,
  What mortal could stand clear!
But there is full remission;
That sinners with contrition
  May to Thy throne draw near.

The Lord's good time abiding,
In His sure word confiding,
  I wait in meek suspense:
Those all the long night waking,
Watch for the morning's breaking
  With longing less intense.

Let Israel wait, unfearing,
Jehovah's kind appearing,
  For Mercy is His name.
With Him is full redemption,
A rich and free exemption
  From sorrow, guilt, and shame.

"Let Israel hope in the Lord, for with the Lord there is mercy."—
Psalm cxxx. 7, 8.

HOPE, ye mourners, in The Lord:
Rest upon His faithful word.
To His mercy have recourse:
He of mercy is the source,
Whence, to heal all human woes,
Plenteous redemption flows.
He from sin, and death, and hell,
Will redeem His Israel.

PSALM CXXXVI.

" O give thanks unto the Lord; for He is good."—Psalm cxxxvi.

To our God loud praises give,
Source of good to all who live.
Praise His name, whose mercy sure
Shall eternally endure.

To The Lord your homage bring,
God of gods, of kings the King.
For His mercy, free and sure,
Shall eternally endure.

Praise Him for His deeds of might,
For His greatness infinite,
For His mercy free and sure,
Which doth evermore endure.

He by wisdom built the skies,
And bade earth from ocean rise;
Filled the sun with glorious light;
Gave the moon to rule the night.

He beheld us when brought low,
And redeemed us from the foe.
He doth every blessing give:
By His bounty all things live.

Oh, give thanks; your voices raise
To the God of heaven in praise,
For His mercy, free and sure,
Shall eternally endure.

"I will extol Thee, my God, O King."—Psalm cxlv.

I WILL extol Thy name, O God my King!
   For ever will I bless Thee; day by day,
Shall my glad lips Thy daily goodness sing,
   To Thee a never-ceasing tribute pay.

Great is Jehovah, infinitely great:
   Exalted as His greatness be His praise.
Fathers to sons Thy wonders shall relate,
   And distant ages learn the song to raise.

Thy glorious majesty shall be my theme;
   And men of all Thy awful deeds shall tell:
I will declare Thy power and rule supreme,
   While they on Thy remembered mercies dwell.

The Lord is gracious, and to wrath how slow!
   Full of compassion, ready to forgive:
The Lord is good: how free His mercies flow!
   His bounty is the life of all that live.

Thee, all Thy works, Maker Omnipotent,
   Through all the various realms of Nature praise:
Thee, all Thy saints, with voice intelligent
   Adoring, sing the wonders of Thy ways.

Oh, let them to an impious world proclaim,
   That glory, power, and government are Thine;
Till earth confess the terrors of Thy name,
   And kings to Thee their shadowy crowns resign.

Thy kingdom is an everlasting reign;
   For ever Thy dominion must extend;
The universe unbounded Thy domain,
   Enduring till Eternity shall end.

Our God is faithful; every word must stand;
   Nor can He change, nor can His promise fail.
The Lord upholds the falling: His own hand
   Raises the prostrate, and supports the frail.

On Thee all creatures wait. Lord! Thou suppliest
   The beasts with food: they cry in their distress;
Thou openest Thy hand and satisfiest
   The wants of all that live with plenteousness.

The Lord is righteous, merciful as just,
   Holy as merciful. The Lord is nigh
To all who call upon His name, and trust
   His mercy: He will surely hear their cry.

No harm can reach His children: they shall see
   The wicked perish, and adore His ways.
My heart shall still exult, O God, in Thee:
   Let every tongue swell Thine eternal praise.

HYMNS

OF

PRAISE AND ADORATION.

HYMNS OF PRAISE AND ADORATION.

"The High and Lofty One who inhabiteth eternity."—Isa. lvii. 15.
"From Him who is, and who was, and who is to come."—Rev. i. 4, 5.

TO Him who is above all height,
Who dwells in uncreated light;
To Him whose Being fills the vast
Eternal Cycle of the Past;
Who, in His Present, comprehends
Futurity that never ends:
  Let thanks and praise resound,
  Wide as Creation's bound.

To Him who formed the heavens and earth,
And gave to all existence birth;
To Him with whom is nothing small,
Who notices the sparrow's fall;
To Him whose condescending grace
Makes humble hearts His dwelling-place;
  Let thanks and praise resound,
  Wide as Creation's bound.

To Him who makes The Father known,
To Him who shares The Father's throne;
In whom His full perfections dwell,
The Image of The Invisible;
The Word before all time began,
The Son of God, the Son of Man;
    Let thanks and praise resound,
    Wide as Creation's bound.

To Him who, by The Father sent,
Deigned to be man, and meekly bent
To human suffering, anguish, death,
Yet, conquered with His dying breath;
Who died to save, who rose to reign,
And who will come in clouds again;
    Let thanks and praise resound,
    Wide as Creation's bound.

To Him who worketh all in all,
Repairer of our nature's fall;
Legate of Him who pleads above,
Dispenser of The Father's love;
Whom One with Both, yet not the same,
We in our faith's confession name;
    Let thanks and praise resound,
    Wide as Creation's bound.

To Heaven's Eternal Majesty,
The Godhead's Trinal Mystery,

Of whom, by whom, and to whom are
All things; whose glory beams from far,
Whose grace is nigh; our Source, our Rest;
God over all, for ever blessed;
    Let thanks and praise resound,
    Through one eternal round.

"Worthy is the Lamb that was slain."—Rev. v. 12.

NOW with angels round the Throne,
   Cherubim and seraphim,
And the Church which still is one,
   Let us swell the solemn hymn:
Glory to the great I AM!
Glory to the Victim-Lamb!

Blessing, honour, glory, might,
And dominion infinite,
To The Father of Our Lord,
To The Spirit and The Word;
As it was all worlds before,
Is, and shall be evermore.

"I am Thine, save me."—Psalm cxix. 94.

CREATOR of all being,
My Maker, God all-seeing,
    My Source, my Rest!
Thy grace in me fulfil;
Re-mould me to Thy will,
    And make me blest.

Redeemer of the lost,
Thy blood the ransom-cost,
    Thy grace afford:
The faith, the virtue give,
On Thee, to Thee to live,
    My Life, my Lord!

Spirit of quickening might,
Fountain of love and light,
    Thyself impart;
And with Thine influence sweet,
Most Blessed Paraclete,
    Possess my heart.

Almighty Father, Word,
And Spirit, each adored,
    In Godhead One!
Throughout creation's frame,
All glory to Thy name:
    Thy will be done.

"Our Father who art in heaven."—Matthew vi. 9.

HEAVENLY FATHER! all things came
From Thy hand, and Thee proclaim:
Hallowed be Thy glorious Name.

Lamb of God, for sinners slain!
O'er Sin's long usurped domain,
Spread Thy all-restoring reign.

Breathe, life-giving Spirit, till,
As the hosts of Heaven fulfil,
Earth shall do her Maker's will.

Father! from whose bounties wide
All Thy creatures are supplied,
For our daily wants provide.

Saviour! cause our hearts to know
Pardoning grace; Thy peace bestow,
As we love and pity shew.

Holy Spirit! led by Thee,
All temptation may we flee:
From all evil set us free.

Glory to The Father's name;
Praise The Lamb with loud acclaim;
To The Paraclete the same:

As ere time began its round,
Now, where'er His saints are found,
And through ages without bound.

"Our Father who art in heaven."—Matt. vi. 9.

FATHER of Spirits! God of heaven!
All glory to Thy name be given.
Thy kingdom come: let earth fulfil,
As do the hosts of heaven, Thy will.

Supply our need; in Thee we live;
And, as we mercy show, forgive.
Preserve us, in temptation's hour,
From sin and every evil power.

For Thine is the dominion; Thine
All power and majesty divine:
Be Thine the glory, as before
All worlds, so, now and evermore.

"Hallowed be thy name."—Matt. vi. 9.

HOLY, holy, holy Lord,
In the highest heavens adored,
Author of all nature's frame;
Father, hallowed be Thy name.

Though estranged from Thee in heart,
Doubtless Thou our Father art:
From Thy hand our spirits came:
Father, hallowed be Thy name.

Nor by nature's tie alone
Thou art as Our Father known:
Nearer now, in Christ, our claim:
Father, hallowed be Thy name.

Born anew, oh, may we feel
Filial love, The Spirit's seal;
Cleansed from guilt, redeemed from shame:
Father, hallowed be Thy name.

Whether, then, in want or wealth,
Joy or sorrow, pain or health,
Still our prayer shall be the same:
Father, hallowed be Thy name.

"Thy will be done."—Matt. vi. 10.

Father of eternal grace!
   Thou hast loved our rebel-race:
Let Thy will, through Christ Thy Son,
As in heaven, on earth be done.

Here, in vain Thy will is known,
Heard in thunder, graved on stone.
By Thy grace Thy will impart:
Write Thy law on every heart.

Let Thy reconciling word
By all tribes of man be heard.
Give the new creation birth:
Let Thy will be done on earth.

"It is He that hath made us."—Psalm c. 3.

OH, give thanks to Him who made
Morning light and evening shade ;
Source and Giver of all good,
Nightly sleep and daily food ;
Quickener of our wearied powers,
Guard of our unconscious hours.

Oh, give thanks to Nature's King,
Who made every breathing thing :
His, our warm and sentient frame,
His, the mind's immortal flame.
Oh, how close the ties that bind
Spirits to the Eternal Mind!

Oh, give thanks with heart and lip,
For we are His workmanship ;
And all creatures are His care :
Not a bird that cleaves the air,
Falls unnoticed ; but who can
Speak The Father's love to man ?

Oh, give thanks to Him who came
In a mortal, suffering frame,—
Temple of the Deity,—
Came for rebel man to die ;
In the path Himself hath trod,
Leading back His saints to God.

"It is a good thing to give thanks unto The Lord."—Psalm xcii. 1.

'TIS good, in tuneful verses,
  Our God's high praise to sing;
The Father of all mercies,
  Our Maker and our King.
We'll praise Him for creation,
  The mercies of our birth;
For daily preservation
  And all the joys of earth.

But, for the great Redemption,
  Let louder anthems swell;
For pardon and exemption
  From woes no tongue can tell.
To Him all glory render,
  Himself who freely gave;
Our Ransom, our Defender,
  Omnipotent to save.

We bless the Holy Spirit,
  For all the means of grace;
The hopes that we inherit,
  The faith that we embrace;
The seal of our high calling,
  The word that makes us wise,
And strength to keep from falling,
  And win the victor's prize.

Oh for a deep impression
  Of mercies numberless,
That, to our lips' profession
  Of constant thankfulness,
Our life may answer truly,
  In grateful service spent:
Then shall we praise Him duly,
  Who life and breath has lent.

DOXOLOGY.

"My mouth shall speak the praise of the Lord."—Psalm cxlv. 21.

PRAISE the God of all creation;
  Praise The Father's boundless love:
Praise The Lamb, our Expiation,
  Priest and King enthroned above:
Praise the Fountain of Salvation,
  Him by whom our spirits live:
Undivided adoration
  To the One Jehovah give.

"Blessed be Thou, Lord God of Israel our Father."—1 Chron. xxix. 10—18.

LORD GOD, our Heavenly Father! be
   Thy name for ever blessed:
Greatness, and power, and majesty
   Are but by Thee possessed.

For all in heaven and earth is Thine:
   O'er all Thy reign extends.
Thy glories through creation shine;
   Thy name all praise transcends.

Riches from Thee, and honour flow;
   Supreme and sovereign Lord!
All power and might Thy hands bestow,
   Strength and success afford.

Therefore with thanks we bow the knee,
   Thy glorious name adore,
Who can but offer unto Thee
   Of what was Thine before.

Strangers and sojourners, we own
   Ourselves and all our race;
Our days on earth a shadow thrown,
   That fades and leaves no trace.

All we can give is from Thy hand;
   Thine is whate'er we hold.
Trier of hearts! by Thy command
   Be every thought controlled.

A free-will offering to Thy name,
   This house, O God, we raise;
Thy grace and truth we here proclaim,
   And here record Thy praise.

"Whither shall I go from Thy Spirit?"—Psalm cxxxix. 7.

BEYOND, beyond that boundless sea,
   Above that dome of sky,
Further than thought itself can flee,
   Thy dwelling is on high:
Yet dear the awful thought to me,
   That Thou, my God, art nigh:—

Art nigh, and yet my labouring mind
   Feels after Thee in vain,
Thee in these works of power to find,
   Or to Thy seat attain.
Thy messenger, the stormy wind;
   Thy path, the trackless main;—

These speak of Thee with loud acclaim;
   They thunder forth Thy praise,—
The glorious honour of Thy name,
   The wonders of Thy ways:
But Thou art not in tempest-flame,
   Nor in day's glorious blaze.

We hear Thy voice, when thunders roll
   Through the wide fields of air:
The waves obey Thy dread control;
   But still, Thou art not there.
Where shall I find Him, O my soul,
   Who yet is everywhere?

Oh, not in circling depth or height,
   But in the conscious breast,
Present to faith, though veiled from sight,
   There doth His Spirit rest.
Oh come, Thou Presence Infinite!
   And make Thy creature blest.

"He left not Himself without witness, in that He ... gave us ... fruitful seasons."—Acts xiv. 17.

O THOU who givest all their food,
   Causing Thy sun to shine
Upon the evil and the good!
   Earth's teeming stores are Thine.

Thy covenant to man secures
   The harvest of his toil:
Thy faithful word, while earth endures,
   With plenty clothes the soil.

The wintry frost, the flowery prime,
   Alike Thy laws obey:
Each herb and blossom knows its time,
   And feels the quickening ray.

Revolving seasons still proclaim
   Thy all-sustaining word:
Seed-time and harvest speak Thy name,
   The promise-keeping Lord.

"His righteousness is unto children's children, to such as keep His covenant."—Psalm ciii. 17, 18.

O THOU whose covenant is sure
   To all who fear Thy name;
Whose mercies age on age endure,
   Eternally the same:
Thou art our fathers' God; we plead
   That title: we are Thine.
Pour down Thy Spirit on our seed,
   And sanctify our line.

In Thee our fathers put their trust;
   Thy ways they humbly trod:
Honoured and sacred is their dust,
   And still they live to God.
Heirs to their faith, their hope, their prayers,
   We the same path pursue.
Entail the blessing to *our* heirs:
   Lord! shew Thy promise true.

"We have known and believed the love that God hath to us. God is love."—1 John iv. 16.

OH, Love beyond the reach of thought,
   That formed the sovereign plan,
Ere Adam had our ruin wrought,
   Of saving fallen Man!
God has so loved our rebel race
   As His own Son to give,
That whoso will, amazing grace!
   May look to Him and live.

Chosen in Christ, His ransomed flock
   The Eternal Purpose prove;
By nature of a sinful stock,
   Made blameless now in love:
Ransomed by price, by blood redeemed,
   Restored by Power Divine,
Though lightly by the world esteemed,
   They as the stars shall shine.

Oh, height of mystery sublime!
   Unfathomed depth of grace!
Length that exceeds the bounds of Time!
   Breadth measureless as space!

Oh for a heart to grasp a theme
  Which knowledge cannot reach!
To unfold Redemption's glorious scheme,
  How weak the power of speech!

Bless'd be The Father of Our Lord,
  From whom all blessings spring!
And bless'd be the Incarnate Word,
  Our Saviour and our King!
We know and have believed the love
  Which God through Christ displays:
And, when we see His face above,
  We'll nobler anthems raise.

"The brightness of His glory and the express image of His person."—Heb. i. 3.

Thou art the Everlasting Word,
   The Father's Only Son;
God manifestly seen and heard,
   And Heaven's Beloved One.
Worthy, O Lamb of God, art Thou,
That every knee to Thee should bow.

In Thee most perfectly expressed,
   The Father's glories shine;
Of the full Deity possessed,
   Eternally Divine.
Worthy, O Lamb of God, art Thou,
That every knee to Thee should bow.

True Image of the Infinite,
   Whose Essence is concealed;
Brightness of Uncreated Light;
   The Heart of God revealed.
Worthy, O Lamb of God, art Thou,
That every knee to Thee should bow.

But the high mysteries of Thy name
   An angel's grasp transcend:
The Father only—glorious claim!—
   The Son can comprehend.

Worthy, O Lamb of God, art Thou,
That every knee to Thee should bow.

Yet, loving Thee, on whom His love
  Ineffable doth rest,
Thy glorious worshippers above,
  As one with Thee, are blest.
Worthy, O Lamb of God, art Thou,
That every knee to Thee should bow.

Throughout the universe of bliss,
  The centre Thou, and sun!
The eternal theme of praise is this,
  To Heaven's Beloved One:—
Worthy, O Lamb of God, art Thou,
That every knee to Thee should bow.

"The faithful Witness, and the First-begotten of the dead, and the Prince of the kings of the earth."—Rev. i. 5.

SUBSTANTIAL Truth, O Christ, Thou art;
 The Witness and the Theme:
The light of life Thou dost impart,
 And by the Truth redeem.
Thee of Thy Church the Only Head,
 Master and Lord we own,
And, by Thy word and Spirit led,
 Will follow Thee alone.

Thou Lamb of God for sinners slain !
 We glorify Thy love;
High-priest in Heaven's eternal fane,
 Our Advocate above.
Now, through Thy rended veil of flesh,
 We dare the Throne draw nigh,
And, sprinkled with Thy blood afresh,
 With boldness Abba cry.

Thou art the King of Glory, Lord
 Of every realm and race;
Omnipotent Thy sovereign word,
 Invincible Thy grace.

Assume Thy universal sway;
  Tread down Thy monster foes:
Let earth as heaven Thy will obey,
  And sin's mad conflict close.

Prophet, Redeemer, Prince supreme,
  In whom all fulness dwells!
Thy praise is heaven's eternal theme;
  Thy love all praise excels.
Worthy art Thou by filial right
  To share The Father's throne:
All creatures own Thy sovereign might:
  Oh, make all hearts Thy own.

"The Lamb of God, which taketh away the sin of the world."—
John i. 29.

LAMB of God, who didst sustain
   The guilt of humankind;
Mercy, through Thy mortal pain,
   Grant us, good Lord, to find.
Wash us from our guilty stain;
   Our ransomed souls from sin release:
Lamb of God, for sinners slain!
   Bestow on us Thy peace.

From Thy Cross, in that dread hour,
   Thou bad'st one sinner live:
From Thy throne, display Thy power
   Pardon and life to give.
Son of God! on Thee we call:
   Save us from guilt and fear and shame.
Lamb of God, and Lord of all!
   We sinners bless Thy name.

"There am I in the midst of them."—Matt. xviii. 20.

WHERESOEVER two or three
    Meet, a Christian company,
Grant us, Lord, to meet with Thee.
               Gracious Saviour, hear!

When with friends beloved we stray,
Talking down the closing day,
Saviour! meet us in the way.
               Gracious Saviour, hear!

When, amid the gloom of night,
Storms arise, and perils fright,
Let Thy voice our hearts delight.
               Gracious Saviour, hear!

In the festive hour, refine
Earthly love to joy divine:
Turn the water into wine.
               Gracious Saviour, hear!

In the time of lonely grief,
Let Thy presence bring relief;
Then shall longest nights grow brief.
               Gracious Saviour, hear!

When the world and life recede,
Saviour! in our hour of need,
Then be visible indeed.
    Gracious Saviour, hear!

"'To me to live is Christ, and to die is gain.'"—Phil. i. 21.

GRANT me, Heavenly Lord! to feel
In thy cause a servant's zeal:
More than all to self most near,
May I hold Thine honour dear;
Willing to forego my pride,
So my Lord be glorified.

In the conquests of Thy might,
May I loyally delight;
In Thy ever-spreading reign,
Triumph as my greatest gain.
Make me conscious, by this sign,
Saviour! Sovereign! I am Thine.

"Come, Lord Jesus!"—Rev. xxii. 20.

COME, Lord Jesus! haste the day
Of Thy universal sway:
Lord of lords, Thy power display.

Come, Lord Jesus! come in light;
With the spirit of Thy might,
All the powers of darkness smite.

From Thy mouth send forth Thy sword,
Thine all-piercing, sovereign word:
Vindicate Thy truth, O Lord!

Not with pomp or martial force,
Prince of Peace, Thy conquering course:
White is Thy triumphal horse.

Not as on that day of dread,
When the trump that wakes the dead,
Shall its awful summons spread.

Not enthroned in dread array,
As when, stricken with dismay,
Heaven and earth shall pass away.

Viewless, make Thy presence felt,
Where the Anti-Christ hath dwelt:
At Thy voice all hearts shall melt.

At Thy voice all realms shall shake,
Earth beneath Thy tread shall quake,
And the slumbering Church awake.

Come, to slay the Man of Sin:
Let the brighter age begin,
Which his fall shall usher in.

Come, that wars and strife may cease;
Come, Thy captive Church release;
Bring the reign of Truth and Peace.

Come, the mystery to fulfil;
Come, that earth may learn Thy will;
Reigning at God's right-hand still:

Reigning there till all Thy foes,
Death the last, Thou shalt depose:
Then shall come the glorious close.

"Who maketh manifest the savour of His knowledge by us in every place."—2 Cor. ii. 4.

O THOU, our Head, enthroned on high,
  By whom Thy members live!
Wilt Thou not hear our fervent cry;
  The holy unction give?
In all the plenitude of grace,
  Thy sevenfold gifts bestow,
And by us, Lord! in every place,
  Thy saving virtue show.

Our Christian land with error teems,
  The blind by blinder led;
The sophist weaves his atheist schemes;
  Wide has the poison spread.
Arise, O Lord! send forth Thy word;
  Thy faithful heralds call;
And, while the Gospel trump is heard,
  Let Satan's bulwarks fall.

Free, pure, and vital as the light,
  God's message to our race;
Like genial gales the Spirit's might,
  Sovereign, mysterious grace.

Breathe forth, O wind,* and to new birth
  Quicken the bones of death:
Regenerate this withered earth;
  Give to the dying, breath.

"The Head from which all the body having nourishment ministered, increaseth with the increase of God."—Col. ii. 19.

HEAD of the Church, our Risen Lord,
  Who by Thy Spirit dost preside
O'er the whole body; by whose word
  They all are ruled and sanctified:

Our prayers and intercessions hear
  For all Thy family at large,
That each, in his appointed sphere,
  His proper service may discharge.

So, through the grace derived from Thee,
  In whom all fulness dwells above,
May Thy whole Church united be,
  And edify itself in love.

* Ezek. xxxvii. 9.

"He shall baptize you with the Holy Ghost, and with fire."—
Matt. iii. 11.

Oh, breathe upon this languid frame,
   Spirit of heavenly might!
Baptize me with the vital flame
   Of purity and light.

Descend like heaven's self-kindled fire
   On my heart's sacrifice,
Till self in flames of love expire,
   In clouds of incense rise.

Spring up within this flinty heart,
   Well-spring of life divine!
Health to my feeble pulse impart:
   Light, out of darkness shine.

O Light and Power! O Life and Love!
   Of every good the Source!
Send me sweet succour from above,
   To speed me on my course.

Instruct me, rule me, guide my feet,
   My every thought control:
My Teacher, Patron, Paraclete!
   Possess and guard my soul.

Spirit of Christ, sent forth from Him,
  Yet uncreate, Divine!
Thine are the songs of Seraphim:
  All human praise be Thine.

"I will not leave you comfortless."—John xiv. 18.

LEAVE us not comfortless,
  O Thou our Risen Lord;
But send Thy Spirit down, to bless
  And guide us with Thy word!
By Him Thy gifts impart,
  Light, peace and joy, and love;
Seal of adoption in our heart,
  Earnest of heaven above.

"Shew me Thy ways, O Lord! Teach me Thy paths."—
Psalm xxv. 4.

O GOD, from whom is my desire
   To know and do Thy will!
That knowledge wilt Thou not inspire,
   That high resolve fulfil?

Thy wise intents, vouchsafe to make
   Thy servant understand:
Show me the path that I should take,
   Led by Thy guiding Hand.

Teach me, amid conflicting views,
   Truth's mystery to discern;
And, while the proud their labour lose,
   Still at Thy feet to learn.

'Mid shifting scenes and portents strange,
   Perplexing courts and schools,
Grant me, unfearing every change,
   To see the Hand that rules:—

To read what Wisdom's pride confounds,
   With Faith's prophetic glance,
And hear, amid discordant sounds,
   Thy chariot-wheels advance.

Teach me what Thou wouldst have me teach;
  Arm me for Truth's defence;
Yet, louder let my conduct preach,
  Than noblest eloquence.

With active hands and willing feet,
  Obedient to Thy rod,
May I stand perfect and complete
  In all the will of God.

"If that I may apprehend that for which also I am apprehended of Christ Jesus."— Phil. iii. 12.

MY LORD! I recognize Thy claim:
  Chosen and called by Sovereign Grace,
Thy purpose shall direct my aim;
  I that whole purpose would embrace,
And for the full reward contend,
Still pressing towards the glorious end.

The Hand that saved, upholds me still,
  And gives me strength for His employ.
Lord! may I finish all Thy will,
  And so complete my course with joy;
Faithful through grace, my high reward,
To share the triumph of my Lord.

"Thou, Lord, art a shield for me; my glory, and the lifter up of my head."—Psalm iii. 3.
"The Lord is my strength and song."—Psalm cxviii. 14.

I AM Thy workmanship, O Lord!
   And unto Thee belong.
Thou art my shield, my great reward,
   My glory and my song.

Surround me with Thy guardian might;
   Uphold me with Thy grace:
Unharmed, conduct me through the fight,
   Unwearied, through the race.

Make me a weapon of Thy power,
   An angel of Thy will:
To Thee devoted, let each hour
   Its happy task fulfil.

Yet dare I not, a child of dust,
   Thus plead my filial claim,
But as in Him is all my trust,
   Who bears a Saviour's name.

"O Lord, Thou hast searched me and known me."—Psalm cxxxix. 1.

Lord! whate'er in mortal eyes
  My conscious soul appear,
Seen beneath that fair disguise
  Which veils the most sincere,
Thou dost, with all-piercing view,
Search my inmost spirit through.

In my native vileness seen,
  Ere Grace subdued my will;
All the sinner might have been,
  All that makes me still
Sigh or tremble, doubt or moan,
Known to Thee, and Thee alone.

In abasement at Thy feet,
  Lord! I would ever lie:
Yet, it is a Mercy-seat,
  And I may venture nigh.
Who the contrite shall condemn?
Christ hath died and pleads for them.

Let me still, in human sight,
  A holy semblance wear.
What but Mercy Infinite
  Could perfect knowledge bear?

He who fashioned, knows my frame,
And Forgiveness is His name.

But, if Thine approving smile,
   My Father, cheer my breast,
Let the world account me vile,
   It shall not break my rest.
Strong in weakness I shall be;
Rich, however poor, in Thee.

"I was brought low, and He helped me."—Psalm cxvi. 6.

O THOU GOD who hearest prayer,
Every hour and every where!
Listen to my feeble breath,
Now I touch the gates of death.
For His sake whose blood I plead,
Hear me in the hour of need.

Hear and save me, gracious Lord!
For my trust is in Thy word.
Wash me from the stain of sin,
That Thy peace may rule within.
May I know myself Thy child,
Ransomed, pardoned, reconciled.

Dearest Lord! may I so much
As Thy garment's hem but touch:
Or but raise my languid eye
To the cross where Thou didst die;
It shall make my spirit whole;
It shall heal and save my soul.

Thou art merciful to save:
Thou hast snatched me from the grave.
I would kiss the chastening rod,
O my Father and my God!

Only hide not now Thy face,
God of all-sufficient grace!

Leave me not, my Strength, my Trust!
Oh, remember I am dust.
Leave me not again to stray;
Leave me not the tempter's prey.
Fix my heart on things above:
Make me happy in Thy love.

"My soul is even as a weaned child."—Psalm cxxxi. 2.

YES, my God, Thy will is best:
On Thy faithfulness I rest.
Gently wean me from my will,
Yet, with love sustain me still;
That, for Thy denials kind,
I sweet recompence may find,
In the beamings of Thy face,
In robuster growth of grace.

"God is light; and in Him is no darkness at all."—1 John i. 5.

OH for the spirit of a child,
  A heart entirely reconciled
    To Thee and to Thy will,
Most blessèd God! and, springing thence,
A stedfast, loving confidence,
    All restless thoughts to still!

And can a doubt this truth obscure,
That God is light, from darkness pure,
    Love joined with Power supreme?
Where, then, could hope or reason rest?
But in this knowledge I am blessed:
    To doubt were to blaspheme.

This faith of love, O God, impart,
That I may joy in all Thou art,
    And all Thou art adore:
So shall this be my constant song;
God is, and I to God belong,
    My God for evermore.

"If any man serve me, let him follow me."—John xii. 26.

How shall I follow Him I serve?
  How shall I copy Him I love?
Nor from those blessed footsteps swerve,
  Which lead me to His seat above?

Privations, sorrows, bitter scorn,
  The life of toil, the mean abode,
The faithless kiss, the crown of thorn,
  Are these the consecrated road?

'Twas thus He suffered, though a Son,
  Foreknowing, choosing, feeling all;
Until the perfect work was done,
  And drunk the bitter cup of gall.

Lord! should my path through suffering lie,
  Forbid it I should e'er repine.
Still let me turn to Calvary,
  Nor heed my griefs, remembering Thine.

Oh, let me think how Thou didst leave
  Untasted every pure delight,
To fast, to faint, to watch, to grieve,
  The toilsome day, the homeless night:—

To faint, to grieve, to die for me!
   Thou camest not Thyself to please.
And, dear as earthly comforts be,
   Shall I not love Thee more than these?

Yes, I would count them all but loss,
   To gain the notice of Thine eye.
Flesh shrinks and trembles at the cross,
   But Thou canst give the victory.

Thou who for Peter's faith didst pray!
   Against whose blessed self were hurled
The tempter's darts! be Thou my stay:
   Help me to overcome the world.

Thy grace can make the boastful meek,
   The wavering firm, the sensual pure,—
Put heavenly might upon the weak,
   And make them happy who endure.

Oh, still that needful grace afford:
   On Thee my trembling soul I cast.
Perfect Thy work within me, Lord!
   And own my worthless name at last.

[In the Congregational Hymn Book, the last three stanzas are printed as a separate Hymn.]

"Nevertheless I am continually with Thee."—Psalm lxxiii. 23–26.

WHEN, in the hour of lonely woe,
   I give my sorrows leave to flow,
And anxious fear and dark distrust
Weigh down my spirit to the dust;—

When not even friendship's gentle aid
Can heal the wounds the world has made;—
Oh, this shall check each rising sigh,
My Saviour is for ever nigh!

His counsels and upholding care
My safety and my comfort are:
And He shall guide me all my days,
Till glory crown the work of grace.

Jesus! in whom but Thee above,
Can I repose my trust, my love?
And shall an earthly object be
Loved in comparison with Thee?

My flesh is hastening to decay:
Soon shall the world have passed away:
And what can mortal friends avail,
When heart, and strength, and life shall fail?

But oh, be Thou, my Saviour, nigh,
And I will triumph while I die.
My strength, my portion, is Divine;
And Jesus is for ever mine.

"Ye have not chosen me, but I have chosen you."—John xv. 16.

'TIS not that I did choose Thee,
  For, Lord! that could not be:
This heart would still refuse Thee,
  But Thou hast chosen me;—
Hast, from the sin that stained me,
  Washed me and set me free,
And to this end ordained me,
  That I should live to Thee.

'Twas Sovereign Mercy called me,
  And taught my opening mind;
The world had else enthralled me,
  To heavenly glories blind.
Thy grace, my young heart guiding,
  Infixed me in the Root,
In which by faith abiding,
  I bear my humble fruit.

Truly I am Thy servant;
  By birth, by ransom Thine.
Oh, that with zeal more fervent,
  I made Thy pleasure mine!
My heart owns none above Thee;
  For Thy rich grace I thirst;
This knowing, if I love Thee,
  Thou must have loved me first.

"He was known of them in breaking of bread."—Luke xxiv. 35.

FAR from my thoughts, vain world, depart:
Make not the house of prayer thy mart.
Lord of the temple and the day!
Drive the intrusive crowd away.

Fain would I find a calm retreat
From vain distractions near Thy feet,
And, borne above all earthly care,
Be joyful in Thy house of prayer.

Lord! in this blest and hallowed hour,
Reveal Thy presence and Thy power.
Shew to my faith Thy hands and side,
My Lord and God, the Crucified!

Or let me, through the opening skies,
Catch one bright glimpse of Paradise;
And realize, with raptured awe,
The vision dying Stephen saw.

But, if unworthy of such joy,
Still shall Thy love my heart employ:
For, of thy favoured children's fare,
'Twere bliss the very crumbs to share.

Yet, never can my soul be fed
With less than Thee, the Living Bread.
Thyself unto my soul impart,
And with Thy presence fill my heart.

"I am the living bread which came down from heaven."—John vi. 51.

BREAD of Heaven! on Thee I feed,
For Thy flesh is meat indeed.
Ever may my soul be fed
With this true and living bread:
Day by day with strength supplied,
Through the life of Him who died.

Vine of Heaven! Thy blood supplies
This blest cup of sacrifice.
'Tis Thy wounds my healing give:
To Thy cross I look, and live.
Thou my life! Oh, let me be
Rooted, grafted, built on Thee.

"Let a man examine himself, and so let him eat of that bread."—
1 Cor. xi. 28.

O THOU Divine High Priest!
   To Thee I lift mine eyes:
Admit me to the blessed feast
   Of Thine own sacrifice.

   Break Thou to me the bread,
   Type of Thy bruised frame.
Give me to hope that Thou hast bled
   To save my soul from shame.

   Lord! while this cup goes round,
   My inmost spirit try.
Can there be here one traitor found?
   Oh say, Lord, is it I?

   Horror is in that thought.
   Lord of all grace and might,
Who with Thy blood my soul hast bought!
   Assert, secure Thy right.

   Save me, for I am Thine:
   Forgive, accept me now:
And let this sacred bread and wine
   Seal and insure my vow.

"The Lord answered him not; neither by dreams nor by Urim, nor by prophets."—1 Sam. xxviii. 6.

O GOD, who didst Thy will unfold
　In wondrous modes to saints of old,
By dream, by oracle, or seer!
Wilt Thou not still Thy people hear?

What though no answering voice is heard;
Thine oracles, the written word,
Counsel and guidance still impart,
Responsive to the upright heart.

What though no more by dreams is shewn,
That future things to God are known;
Enough the promises reveal:
Wisdom and love the rest conceal.

Faith asks no signal from the skies,
To shew that prayers accepted rise:
Our Priest is in the holy place,
And answers from the throne of grace.

No need of prophets to inquire:
The sun is risen; the stars retire.
The Comforter is come, and sheds
His holy unction on our heads.

Lord! with this grace our hearts inspire;
Answer our sacrifice by fire;
And by Thy mighty acts declare,
Thou art the God who heareth prayer.

"Do not abhor us, for Thy name's sake."—Jer. xiv. 21.

LORD, for Thy name's sake! Such the plea,
   With force triumphant fraught,
By which Thy saints prevail with Thee,
   By Thine own Spirit taught.

For this Thou didst existence give
   To nature's wondrous frame;
And all things shine, and breathe, and live,
   To glorify Thy name.

For this the Saviour lived and died,
   That, in a new-born race,
Thy mercy might be glorified,
   Thine all-victorious grace.

Then, for Thy name's sake, O our God,
   Do not abhor our prayer;
But, while we bow beneath Thy rod,
   Thy chastened people spare.

Oh, for Thy name's sake, richly grant
   The unction from above:
Fulfil Thy holy covenant,
   And glorify Thy love.

"Even as The Lord the Church."—Eph. v. 29.

O GOD, who didst an equal mate
   For Adam of himself create,
Flesh of his flesh, bone of his bone,
That both might feel and love as one!
Make these Thy servants one in heart:
Whom Thou hast joined, let no man part.

Lord of the Church, whose bleeding side
Gave life to thy redeemed Bride;
Whose grace, through every member spread,
Joins the whole Body to its Head!
Oh, let Thy love the model be,
Of this their nuptial unity.

O Thou who once, a guest Divine,
Didst turn the water into wine!
Thy presence, not unsought, afford;
Fill Thou their cup, and bless their board;
And, while each heart Thy word obeys,
May all their joy be turned to praise.

Spirit of Grace and Holiness,
Who dost these vital frames possess,
As living temples, which to stain,
Were God's own dwelling to profane!
May these Thy servants, honouring Thee,
Be kept in love and purity.

Now, to the undivided Name
The Church adores, her rites proclaim,—
Sealed with the gift of Pentecost;
To Father, Son, and Holy Ghost,
All praise be given; in every state,
Be soul and body consecrate.

THE BENEDICTION.

"The peace of God . . . keep your hearts and minds."—Phil. iv. 7.

THE peace of God, transcending
  All human comprehending,
    Its secret joys afford;
Your heart and mind defending,
In faith and love depending
    On Jesus Christ our Lord.

COLLECTS IN VERSE.

COLLECTS IN VERSE.

"For this purpose the Son of God was manifested; that he might destroy the works of the devil."—1 John iii. 8.

O GOD, whose blessed Son as man appeared,
    The power and works of Satan to destroy,
That we, enfranchised from his thrall and cleared
    From guilt, might rise to Heaven's eternal joy!
Grant that, this hope within our hearts made sure,
We may in life be as our Saviour pure:

That, when He shall return, in clouds descending,
    Not as at first, in low and humble guise,
But clad in glory, Heaven's bright hosts attending,
    We, changed into His likeness, may arise
To meet Him where, O Father, one with Thee,
And Thee, O Holy Ghost, He reigns eternally.

"Because Christ suffered for us, leaving us an example that ye should follow His steps."—1 Pet. ii. 21.

O GOD, who didst for man's salvation
   Thy Son to suffering give,
To make for sin propitiation,
   And shew us how to live!
Grant that, most thankfully embracing
   That grace so rich, so free,
We may, the Saviour's footsteps tracing,
   His faithful followers be,
   Through Him who reigns with Thee.

"I have no pleasure in the death of the wicked."—Ezek. xxxiii. 11.

ETERNAL GOD, who hatest
   No work that Thou createst;
Who grantest free remission
To all who feel contrition!
Make these hard hearts relenting,
That we, our sins lamenting,
Our wretchedness deploring,
Thy boundless grace adoring,
May peace divine inherit,
Through our Redeemer's merit.

"Baptized into His death."—Rom. vi. 3.

BAPTIZED into our Saviour's death,
Who for our sins gave up His breath,
Lord! grant us grace from day to day,
Our baser tendencies to slay.

Entombed with Him, our risen Head,
May we to sin and sense be dead;
And, passing through death's gate, the grave,
Our joyful resurrection have:

Through Him who died, and buried lay,
And rose upon the appointed day;
Thy blessed Son, our glorious Lord:
For ever be His name adored.

"And, having done all, to stand."—Eph. vi. 13.

THOU knowest, Lord, on every hand,
Are snares and dangers strewed;
So that we cannot always stand
In fearless rectitude:
Strengthen our hearts with heavenly might,
All foes and ills to face,
And through temptations life-long fight
Conduct us by Thy grace.

"According to the power that worketh in us."—Eph. i. 20.

O GOD, whose sovereign power and skill
   Can order and control
The hearts of men,—the unruly will
   And passions of the soul!

Make us whate'er Thy laws require
   With filial hearts to love;
What Thou hast promised, to desire
   All earthly things above:

That so, amid this changeful scene,
   Faith may our hearts assure,
Fixed on the hope of joys serene,
   Unfading and secure.

"For it is God who worketh in you both to will and to do of His good pleasure."—Phil. ii. 13.

O GOD, who art the strength of all
   Who place in Thee their trust!
Before Thy throne of grace we fall:
   Thou knowest we are dust;—

Without Thy Spirit, impotent
   To will or act aright:
Change by Thy grace our sinful bent,
   And grant us heavenly might:

That, to Thy precepts giving heed,
   Which bring their own reward,
Thee we may please in will and deed,
   Through Jesus Christ our Lord.

"*While we look not at the things which are seen.*"—2 Cor. iv. 18.

O GOD, Protector of the lowly,
   Of all that trust in Thee;
Without whom nothing strong or holy,
   And nothing good can be!
Guide Thou our steps to heavenly glory,
   And teach us so to choose,
As not for pleasures transitory
   Eternal bliss to lose.

"The Head of all principality and power."—Col. ii. 10.

GRANT, O Saviour, to our prayers,
That this changeful world's affairs,
Ordered by Thy governance,
May so peaceably advance,
That Thy Church, with ardour due,
May her proper work pursue,
In all godly quietness,
Through the Name we ever bless.

"Neither have entered into the heart of man, the things which God hath prepared for them that love Him."—1 Cor. ii. 9.

O GOD, who hast such bliss prepared,
To be by all who love Thee shared,
As mortal man would grasp in vain;
Make our cold hearts to know this love,
That, loving Thee all things above,
We may Thy promises obtain,
Which all we can desire transcend,
And praise and serve Thee without end,
Through Jesus Christ our Lord. Amen.

"Kept by the power of God through faith unto salvation."—
1 Pet. i. 5.

LORD of all power and might,
   All-potent to deliver;
In goodness infinite,
   Of every good the Giver!

Teach us to love Thy name;
   Make grace within us flourish:
Our languid zeal inflame;
   With truth our spirits nourish.

Of Thy great mercy kept,
   By faith, unto salvation,
Through Jesus Christ accept
   Our song of adoration.

"The Lord bless thee and keep thee."—Numb. vi. 24.

O GOD, whose never-failing providence
   Orders, controls all things on high, below:
Be Thou against all evil our defence;
   All needful good for Jesus' sake bestow.

"So run that ye may obtain."—1 Cor. ix. 24.

O GOD, who dost Thy sovereign might
   And high prerogative
Most chiefly shew in thy delight
   To pity and forgive!
Vouchsafe the aid Thy grace supplies,
   So in Thy ways to run,
That we may win the heavenly prize,
   Through Jesus Christ, Thy Son.

"And now abideth faith, hope, charity, these three."—1 Cor. xiii. 13.

ETERNAL FATHER, God of Peace!
   Grant us the spirit to increase
  In faith, in hope, in love:
Make us, that we the prize may gain,
Delight in all Thy laws ordain,
  Through Him who pleads above.

"The Spirit also helpeth our infirmities."—Rom. viii. 26.

SINCE, gracious God! apart from Thee,
  We are but impotence,
Nor to Thyself can pleasing be,
  Till Thou Thy grace dispense :
Grant us Thy Spirit as our guide,
  Charge of our hearts to take,
And over all our thoughts preside,
  For Christ Our Saviour's sake.

"Being justified by faith, we have peace with God."—Rom. v. 1.

TO all Thy faithful people, Lord!
  Pardon and peace impart;
And by Thy Spirit shed abroad
  Thy love in every heart;
That they, from conscious guilt made clean,
May serve Thee with a mind serene.

"One body and one spirit."—Eph. iv. 4.

O GOD, whose grace has knit in one communion
    The body mystical of Christ our Head!
Grant us the grace to keep the Spirit's union,
    One with the living Church and sainted dead:
So may we come at last with them to share
    Those joys ineffable, the free reward
Of all who love Thee, which the heavens prepare,
    Through the redeeming grace of Christ our Lord.

"Whose faith follow."—Heb. xiii. 7.

O GOD, to whom the happy dead
    Still live, united to their Head,
      Their Lord and ours the same!
For all Thy saints, to memory dear,
Departed in Thy faith and fear,
      We bless Thy holy name.

By the same grace upheld, may we
So follow those who followed Thee,
      As with them to partake
The free reward of heavenly bliss.
Merciful Father! grant us this,
      For our Redeemer's sake.

HYMNS
FOUNDED ON
PASSAGES OF HOLY SCRIPTURE.

HYMNS

FOUNDED ON

PASSAGES OF HOLY SCRIPTURE.

"Fear not, Abraham: I am thy shield, and thy exceeding great reward."—Gen. xv. 1.

THY voice, O Lord, I hear not;
  In gloom my path is hid:
Oh, say unto me, Fear not;
  My anxious doubts forbid.
'Mid cold or hostile strangers,
  Be Thou my friend, O Lord!
My shield against all dangers,
  My infinite Reward.

Oh, if, for some wise reason,
  My strength of faith to test,
Thick darkness for a season
  My troubled mind invest;

By some resplendent token,
　Thy presence then reveal:
Confirm what Thou hast spoken,
　And the rich promise seal.

To have the blessed assurance
　That Abraham's God is mine,
Were worth a long endurance
　Of discipline Divine.
Yes, through the intercession
　Of Abraham's Son and Lord,
Secure is Faith's possession,
　And glorious its reward.

"That I may know what more the Lord will say unto me."—
Numb. xxii. 19.

NOT Thy permission, Lord, I ask;
   Thy pleasure I would know;
To do Thy will my daily task,
   And on Thine orders go.

Oh, give me not my heart's desire,
   If that desire offend;
Nor grant me blessings in Thine ire,
   That to my hurt would tend.

I dare not urge the blind request
   Of avarice or pride,
Nor from Thy hand the favour wrest,
   By wiser Love denied.

Let then the world its wages keep;
   Poor is its best reward:
I envy not the miser's heap,
   But wait on Thee, O Lord!

"Get thee up into this mount Abarim, and see the land which I have given unto the children of Israel."—Numb. xxvii. 12.

O LORD! I ask not for the sight
   Of Canaan's happy land,
To wing my spirit for the flight
   To joys at Thy right-hand.

When all the powers of nature fail,
   And the last foe draws near,
One sight alone can then avail
   To banish every fear:

The sight of Him in whom I trust,
   The vision Stephen had,
Of Him whose voice can raise this dust,
   In deathless glory clad.

To know I have in Him believed,
   And am through Him forgiven,—
To be by Him I love received,—
   Oh, this shall be my heaven.

Then tell me not of golden towers,
   Or seas of heavenly rest:
Faith asks not Fancy's graphic powers;
   To love is to be blessed.

I know He has prepared a place,
   Where all His saints shall meet;
I know I shall behold His face,
   And worship at His feet.

"If from thence thou shalt seek the Lord thy God."—Deut. iv. 29.

EXILE who, on foreign strand,
   Dost feel thy bosom swell,
Thinking of thy father-land,
   Where friends and kindred dwell.
If from thence thou seek The Lord,
   Thy Father's God is present there:
Hear Him speaking in His word;
   Approach; He heeds thy prayer.

Wanderer in the ways of sin,
   Who, filled with bitterness,
Dost with contrite heart begin
   Thy misery to confess:
If from thence thou seek The Lord,
   E'en from the depths of thy despair,
Hear the promise of His word:
   Seek; thou shalt find Him there.

"Ye are not as yet come to the rest and to the inheritance."—
Deut. xii. 9.

OH, say not, think not in thy heart,
   I here will take my rest:
Remember, thou a pilgrim art,
   A sojourner confessed.

Think of thy dwelling as a tent,
   Thy business is—advance.
But foes on robbing thee are bent,
   Of thine inheritance.

Remember, then, thy heavenly birth:
   Despise the worldling's frown;
Nor let this meretricious earth
   Beguile thee of thy crown.

Yield not to dull and slumbrous ease,
   The prize, thy life, at stake.
Repose is danger; sleep, disease;
   And few that slumber wake.

'Tis immortality we seek,—
   A free, yet rich reward.
But sin is strong, and flesh is weak:
   Increase our faith, O Lord!

"If the Lord were pleased to kill us ... neither would He have shewed us all these things."—Judges xiii. 23.

IF The Lord had felt displeasure,
   No such wonders He had shewn.
God is gracious beyond measure,
   Where He makes His glories known.

Unbelief is human blindness :—
   Think of all His mercies past,—
Of His providential kindness ;—
   Will He then forsake at last?

Firm the promise He has spoken ;
   In the One Great Sacrifice,
Faith beholds the wondrous token
   That our prayers accepted rise.

"Because I saw that thou camest not within the appointed time."
1 Sam. xiii. 11.

GOD'S good time with patience wait:
Heavenly aid ne'er comes too late.
Fret not at the Lord's delay;
Dare not rashly disobey.

God's good path with courage keep,
Rugged though it be, and steep;
'Tis the safe, the nearest road,
Leading to His high abode.

God's good Word thy manual make;
Let thy trust no sophist shake;
'Tis thy lamp, thy sword, thy chart,
Balm and manna for the heart.

God's good will is always best:
Here with firm assurance rest.
Those who on His love depend,
Have Omnipotence their friend.

"Who giveth songs in the night."—Job xxxv. 10.

WHEN, courting slumber,
    The hours I number,
And sad cares cumber
    My wearied mind;
This thought shall cheer me,
That Thou art near me;
Thine ear to hear me
    Is still inclined.

My soul Thou keepest,
Who never sleepest:
'Mid gloom the deepest,
    There's light above.
Thine eyes behold me;
Thine arms enfold me;
Thy Word has told me,
    That God is Love.

"Bless the Lord, ye His angels, that excel in strength."—
Psalm ciii. 20.

ANGELS, ye who ne'er can know
  Aught that sinks our hearts below,
Mars our music, chains our tongue:
With your high, immortal powers,
  With your harps for ever strung,
Praise your glorious Lord and ours.

Not to your bright hosts belong
Higher themes of grateful song:
  Not to your exalted race
Such mysterious mercy came:
  Yet, you hailed the wondrous grace,
And adored our Saviour's name.

Let Him not those praises lose,
Which ungrateful men refuse.
  Praise Him, Heaven! for earth is mute;
Or is loud in groans and cries,—
  Sounds that ill with praises suit.
Praise Him, O ye happier skies!

In this low and grosser air,
All our breath exhales in prayer:

Wants and woes, and hopes and fears,
Still our joyous thanks repress:
  In your bright, untroubled spheres,
Ye have but to serve and bless.

Oft, when praises I would bring,
Tears will gush forth as I sing:
  Then, the gratitude I feel,
Makes me long for coming days,
  When with all an angel's zeal,
I shall hymn my Saviour's praise.

"Make straight in the desert a highway for our God."—Isa. xl. 3.

CHURCHES of Christ, by God's right-hand
Thick-planted in this favoured land,
If to your hearts His Word be dear,
Oh, think of those who pine to hear,
Far from their native shores exiled,
A pastor's voice amid the wild.

Oh, let a voice of comfort bless
The lone and rugged wilderness.
Send faithful shepherds forth, to feed
The scattered wanderers in their need.
Straight paths for feeble knees prepare;
And drooping hands sustain by prayer.

The heathen, who in darkness lay,
Wake to the dawn of heavenly day:
But shall a worse than pagan night
O'ertake the race that dwelt in light,
And Britain's God, to Britons thrown
On distant shores, become unknown?

Great Shepherd of the ransom'd seed!
For Thy dispersed ones we plead.
How shall these multitudes be fed?
'Tis Thine to multiply the bread.
Richly hast Thou our wants supplied:
By us, for them, for all, provide.

' And call the Sabbath a delight, the holy of the Lord, honourable."
Isa. lviii 13.

  D<small>AY</small> ever bless'd,
   Thy light, thy rest,
I hail with glad emotion;
  Ordained for man,
  When Time began,
For solace and devotion.

  Day more endeared
  Since Christ appeared,
The Life and Resurrection.
  That morning's rays
  Shed o'er these days
His glory's bright reflection.

  Gain's sordid strife,
  Toil's o'erstrained life,
Are now awhile suspended.
  E'en serf and slave
  Brief respite have,
And mourn the Sabbath ended.

  Through all the day,
  Prayers wing their way,

The Throne of Grace addressing;
  With thousand songs,
  From holy throngs,
Returned in showers of blessing.

  Now spreads around
  The joyful sound,
The dead to life awaking;
  The poor, the sad,
  Are now made glad,
Of Mercy's feast partaking.

  Sweet Sabbath hours!
  Time's golden flowers,
With balm and incense freighted:
  Throughout the week,
  Of Heaven they speak,
And things to Heaven related.

  In union sweet,
  Fond circles meet,
And home becomes still dearer,
  As earthly ties
  Catch Hope's bright dyes,
And Heaven itself seems nearer.

  Day ever bless'd!
  Type of the rest

That for the saints remaineth ;
    Happy is he
    Who joys in thee,
And ne'er thy hours profaneth

"For He doth not afflict willingly."—Lam. iii. 33.

BLESSED be God! He is not strict,
    Our follies to requite.
He doth not willingly afflict,
    Or in our groans delight.

With long forbearance He endures
    Those who His wrath defy ;
While to His saints the Cross secures
    A glorious amnesty.

Despise not, then, His chastening,
    Nor faint beneath His rod :
Errands of love our trials bring,
    To lead us back to God.

Good Lord! our doubts and murmurs chase,
    That we may look above ;
And where Thy ways we cannot trace,
    Still trust Thy covenant love.

"And the Lord God shall give unto Him the throne of His father David."—Luke i. 32.

Now is born the promised child;
   Lo! to us is given the Son!
Wonderful, His name is styled;
   Word of God, Almighty One;
King of Glory, Prince of Peace,
Whose dominion ne'er shall cease.

David's Son and David's Lord,
   He who liveth, yet was dead,
Reigns, fulfilled the Angel's word,
   Zion's King, the Church's Head;
Antitype of all foreshewn
By the Temple and the Throne.

He has fixed His court on high,
   Worshipped there in rapturous strains;
Angels on His errands fly:
   There o'er earth and heaven He reigns.
Cast away the Jewish leaven:
Saints, your city is in heaven.

"Now lettest Thou Thy servant depart in peace."—Luke ii. 29.

UPON a world of guilt and night,
    The Morning-star arose.
"Enough! mine eyes have seen its light;
    Now welcome death's repose."

Prophetic joy those words inspired,
    When, in the Virgin's Son,
Simeon beheld the long-desired,
    And blessed God's Holy One.

"Now lettest Thou Thy servant, Lord,
    In peace his soul resign;
These eyes, according to Thy word,
    See Judah's Day-star shine:

"The Light of life, whose healing ray
    Shall sin's deep shades dispel;
To Gentile lands salvation's day;
    Thy glory, Israel!"

Faith still beholds her risen Lord,
    Though hid from mortal sight.
Shine forth, O Saviour, in Thy word,
    And fill the world with light.

"Now is the Son of Man glorified."—John xiii. 31.

THE Cross, the Cross on which He died—
There was the Saviour glorified.
'Twas there our ransom-price He paid,
And of the Cross an altar made,
Self-offered; with His dying breath
Abolishing the power of Death.

That hour of darkness, anguish, strife,
Won for His saints eternal life.
That hour, the Prince of Darkness fell;
That hour foiled all the arts of hell.
The incense of that sacrifice
Opened the gates of Paradise.

The Cross on which the Saviour died,
There was The Father glorified.
There heaven and earth beheld with awe,
Repaired the honour of the law;
And what Eternal Love had willed
To save a guilty world, fulfilled.

Oh, blessed Root, salvation's source,
Uniting, by attractive force,

Around one centre, in one head,
All those for whom the Saviour bled.
Be this our boast, and nought beside,
The Cross where He was glorified.

"He is not here; He is risen. Come, see the place where the
Lord lay."—Matt. xxviii. 6.

OH, shew me not my Saviour dying,
  As on the Cross he bled;
Nor in the tomb, a captive lying,
  For He has left the dead.
Then bid me not that form extended
  For my Redeemer own,
Who, to the highest heavens ascended,
  In glory fills the throne.

Weep not for Him at Calvary's station;
  Weep only for Thy sins.
View where He lay with exultation;
  'Tis there our hope begins.
Yet stay not there, thy sorrows feeding,
  Amid the scenes He trod:
Look up and see Him interceding
  At the right-hand of God.

Still in the shameful Cross I glory,
  Where His dear blood was spilt;
For there the Great Propitiatory
  Abolished all my guilt.

Yet what, 'mid conflict and temptation,
  Shall strength and succour give?
He lives, the Captain of Salvation;
  Therefore His servants live.

By death, He death's dark king defeated,
  Aud overcame the grave:
Rising, the triumph He completed;
  He lives, He reigns to save.
Heaven's happy myriads bow before Him:
  He comes, the Judge of men;
These eyes shall see Him and adore Him;
  Lord Jesus! own me then.

*" He is not here; He is risen. Come, see the place where the
Lord lay."—Matt. xxviii. 6.*

CHRIST our Lord arose to-day:
Come, the empty tomb survey.
Death could not Our Life imprison:
Hallelujah! Christ is risen.

Hence with gloom and rigid fast,
That Sabbatic shadow past:
Now our festal day begins:
Christ hath borne away our sins.

Yea, hath passèd through the sky:
Our High Priest is throned on high.
There His finished work He pleads;
There for ever intercedes.

What can sever from His love?
Nought on earth and nought above.
Those who to the Lamb belong,
All shall learn the conqueror's song.

Blessèd be The Father's name!
Jesus from The Father came.
God, who raised Him from the dead,
Gave us life in Him our Head.

Glory to Th' Incarnate Word,
Who His Spirit has conferred!
Grateful praise and honours meet
To the Blessed Paraclete.

> 'He came unto His own, and His own received Him not."—
> John i. 11.

TO His own world He came;
  To earth's most favoured spot;
Jesus, Immanuel, His name;
  Yet, Israel knew Him not.

Son of The Father's love,
  Effulgence of His light,
He left His glorious court above,
  To suffer man's despite.

He came to suffer death,
  And, bleeding for His foes,
Spoke pardon with His dying breath,
  And peace when He arose.

His latest moments here
  In benediction passed.
To those who saw Him disappear,
  That action was His last.

But, having reached His throne,
  He sent down from above
His promised Spirit, to make known
  The riches of His love.

Ye who have felt that flame,
  On whom that grace is poured,
Go, in His Spirit to proclaim
  Salvation in the Lord.

"Great is the mystery of godliness."—1 Tim. iii. 16.

OH, mystery transcending thought,
  By prophets and apostles taught!
  Here, all our powers adore:
God was made manifest in Man:
The Word, who was ere time began,
  Our mortal nature wore.

He came to make The Father known:
Through all His works the Godhead shone,
  Omnipotent, benign:
The Cross His power to save expressed;
He rose in majesty confessed,
  In spirit all divine.

Angels, who hailed His wondrous birth,
Attended all His steps on earth;
  With awe and glad surprise,
They saw the tempter's malice foiled,
Death vanquished, and the grave despoiled;
  They saw the conqueror rise.

To Roman, Syrian, Arab, Greek,
The very Cross was made to speak

    Messiah's royal claim:
And Gentiles came from far and heard,
Beheld His works, received His word,
    And glorified His name.

By faithless Judah not received,
On Him the wondering world believed;
    Like light His kingdom spread.
Assembled round their Risen Lord,
Numbers beheld Him, and adored,
    The First-born from the dead.

Not long must earth her Lord detain.
Lo! He ascends as Son to reign
    Upon The Father's throne:
There, Priest and King abiding still,
He comes, His promise to fulfil,
    When all His power shall own.

' It is written again, Thou shalt not tempt the Lord thy God."—
Matt. iv. 7.

ART thou a scholar of the word?
 Then must thou meekly learn
To trust, but not to tempt The Lord,
 And faith's true course discern.

Trust Him thy feet to guide and keep,
 Where duty bids thee go;
But not in any venturous leap,
 When conscience whispers No!

Trust Him to give thee good success
 In all thy lawful toil;
But not thy selfish schemes to bless,
 Or the forbidden spoil.

Trust Him for aid and influence,
 Thy worthy aims to win;
But not to make His providence
 Conducive to thy sin.

Trust Him in dark temptation's hour,
 But from temptation flee.
Oh, trust His wisdom, truth, and power,
 Yet wait His work to see.

Lord! I am erring, sinful, weak:
  May not I trust Thee still?
'Tis free, abounding grace I seek,
  While bowing to Thy will.

The prayer that man would coldly spurn,
  With Heaven shall have success.
Blessed be God, who does not turn
  His ear from my distress.

"Give us day by day our daily bread."—Matt. vi. 11.

Day by day the manna fell:
  Oh, to learn this lesson well!
Still, by constant mercy fed,
Give me, Lord, my daily bread.

"Day by day," the promise reads;
Daily strength for daily needs.
Cast foreboding fears away:
Take the manna of to-day.

Lord, my times are in Thy hand.
All my sanguine hopes have planned
To Thy wisdom I resign,
And would make Thy purpose mine.

Thou my daily task shalt give:
Day by day to Thee I live:
So shall added years fulfil,
Not my own, my Father's will.

Fond ambition, whisper not;
Happy is my humble lot.
Anxious, busy cares, away;
I'm provided for to-day.

Oh, to live exempt from care,
By the energy of prayer;
Strong in faith, with mind subdued,
Yet, elate with gratitude!

"Forgive us our debts, as we forgive our debtors."—Matt. vi. 12.

FATHER! to Thy sinful child,
　Though Thy law is reconciled,
By Thy pardoning grace I live;
Daily still I cry, Forgive.

Though my ransom-price He paid,
Upon whom my guilt was laid,
Humbly at Thy mercy-seat,
Full remission I entreat.

Lord, forgive me, day by day,
Debts I cannot hope to pay;
Duties I have left undone;
Evils I have failed to shun;

Trespasses in word or thought;
Deeds from evil motive wrought;
Cold ingratitude, distrust;
Thoughts unhallowed and unjust.

Pardon, Lord! and are there those
Who my debtors are, or foes?
I, who by forgiveness live,
Here their trespasses forgive.

May I feel, beneath my wrongs,
Vengeance to The Lord belongs;
Nor a worse requital dare,
Than the meek revenge of prayer.

Much forgiven, may I learn
Love for hatred to return;
Then assured my heart shall be,
Thou, my God, hast pardoned me.

"And lead us not into temptation, but deliver us from evil."
Matt. vi. 13.

HEAVENLY Father! to whose eye
Future things unfolded lie,
Through the desert where I stray,
Let Thy counsels guide my way.

Lead me not, for flesh is frail,
Where fierce trials would assail:
Leave me not, in darkened hour,
To withstand the tempter's power.

Save me from his treacherous wiles:
Arm me against pleasure's smiles.
Give me, for my spirit's health,
Neither poverty nor wealth.

Help Thy servant to maintain
A profession free from stain;
That my sole reproach may be,
Following Christ and fearing Thee.

Lord! uphold me day by day:
Shed a light upon my way:
Guide me through perplexing snares:
Care for me in all my cares.

All I ask for is—enough.
Only, when the way is rough,
Let Thy rod and staff impart
Strength and courage to my heart.

Should Thy wisdom, Lord! decree
Trials long and sharp for me,
Pain or sorrow, care or shame,
Father! glorify Thy name.

Let me neither faint nor fear,
Feeling still that Thou art near;
In the course my Saviour trod,
Tending still to Thee, my God.

"Come unto me, all ye that labour and are heavy laden, and I will give you rest."—Matt. xi. 28.

OH comfort to the dreary!
  Oh joy to the oppressed!
Come unto me, ye weary,
  And I will give you rest.
Oh, come in all your weakness,
  Ye sons of guilt and woe:
And learn of Him with meekness,
  Who stooped for us so low.

Ye slaves of servile error,
  Wearied with fruitless pains,
Whose faith is doubt and terror,
  Believe, and lose your chains.
Renounce the superstition
  To Christ's light yoke preferred;
And turn from vain tradition
  To His redeeming word.

Ye who, in hall and college,
  Have vainly toiled to find
The satisfying knowledge
  That heals the aching mind;

By ceaseless doubts molested,
　　Or lost in vain surmise;
Come, of your pride divested,
　　And Christ will make you wise.

Ye who the world have courted,
　　And suffered from its spite;
Ye who with sin have sported,
　　And felt its serpent-bite;
Come learn, your follies quitting,
　　That this world's gain is loss;
To His mild rule submitting,
　　Who bare for you the Cross.

"Enter thou into the joy of thy Lord."—Matt. xxv. 21.

TRANSPORTING thought! The Master's joy,
　His servants' great reward!
How should this hope our hearts employ,
　The Triumph of Our Lord!

When all His ransomed Church shall meet,
　The Living and the Dead,
His work in each and all complete,
　Assembled round their Head:

When the great conflict shall have closed,
　All evil be subdued,
Death, the last enemy, deposed,
　And Nature's self renewed:

When what Eternal Love had willed,
　Shall gloriously appear;
The mystery of God fulfilled,
　His purposes made clear:

When, as the Son of Man surveys
　The harvest of His pains,
Swells forth the universal praise
　In new and rapturous strains.

But Love Divine alone can know
    The fulness of that joy,
Which in the Saviour's heart shall glow,
    And Heaven's new song employ.

Enough, the triumph to partake,
    Our place and portion this:
Full sympathy with Him shall make
    The ecstacy of bliss.

"With men it is impossible, but not with God."—Mark x. 27.

Oh, how shall feeble flesh and blood
   Burst through the bonds of sin?
The holy kingdom of our God,
   What man shall enter in?

Despising all that worldlings love,
   By which the soul's enslaved,
Forsaking all for things above,—
   Oh, who can thus be saved?

He who made all things, He who said,
   "Let there be light," can give
This saving strength, can raise the dead,
   And bid the sinner live.

And will not He who ransomed man,
   A Saviour's work fulfil?
Almighty is His power: He can.
   Boundless His love: He will.

His word, His Spirit, all ensures
   To them who trust His love.
Here, saints, shall victory be yours,
   And crowns of joy above.

"The disciple is not above his master."—Luke vi. 40.

As much have I of worldly good
　　As e'er my Master had:
I diet on as dainty food,
　　And am as richly clad,
Though plain my garb, though scant my board,
As Mary's Son, and nature's Lord.

The manger was His infant-bed;
　　His home, the mountain-cave.
He had not where to lay His head;
　　He borrowed e'en His grave.
Earth yielded Him no resting-spot,—
Her Maker, but she knew Him not.

As much the world's good-will I share,
　　Its favour and applause,
As He whose blessed name I bear,—
　　Hated without a cause;
Despised, rejected, mocked by pride,
Betrayed, forsaken, crucified.

Why should I court my master's foe?
　　Why should I fear its frown?
Why should I seek for rest below,
　　Or sigh for brief renown?—
A pilgrim to a better land,
An heir of joys at God's right-hand.

"Nevertheless, at Thy word I will let down the net."—Luke v. 5.
"But He answered her not a word."—Matt. xv. 23.

LONG have I toiled with hope deferred,
 And toiled in vain; but yet,
Lord, at Thy all-commanding word,
 I will let down the net;
Assured, if Thou the effort bless,
Of an o'erpayment of success.

Lord! I have followed Thee with prayer,
 Thou answering not a word;
Yet will I not of help despair;
 I shall at last be heard,
And bless the gracious Voice that saith,
"Be it according to thy faith."

So dost Thou discipline Thy sons
 In training for the skies:
It is the Lord's beloved ones
 Whose strength of faith He tries,
To separate from dross the gold,
And stamp them with a heavenly mould.

"Lord! even the devils are subject unto us through Thy name."—
Luke x. 18.

THAT Name of Power! which Satan heard,
   And like a meteor fell.
Dark spirits trembled at the word
   That burst their cruel spell.

A Mightier than that mighty one
   Stood by His works revealed,
Who, though not yet upon the throne,
   Had foiled him in the field.

The prince of this world long had held
   Usurped, tyrannic sway:
That Name his impious boast dispelled,
   And bade his powers give way.

'Twas not the Cross, the Gospel, then,
   That wrought these deeds of might:
The force of Truth may vanquish men,
   But not infernal spite.

And still, in realms of pagan night,
   Ere Truth can pierce and spread,
That Name must put the foe to flight,
   Which shakes all hell with dread.

Servants of Christ, who hear His word,
　Your Saviour King proclaim:
That Name shall not in vain be heard:
　Go, triumph in that Name.

Before it every power must fall,
　And wailing demons flee;
For, at the Name of Jesus, all
　That live shall bow the knee.

"A treasure in the heavens that faileth not."—Luke xii. 53.

My wealth is in a world of joy,
   Secured by God's own seal,
Where moth or rust can ne'er destroy,
   Nor thieves break through to steal.

Oh, blessed state, where nought shall be
   Less beauteous than it seems;
Where substance and reality
   Transcend earth's brightest dreams!

There, friends no jealousies divide,
   Warm hearts turn never cold;
There, Envy cannot breathe, nor pride,
   And nothing fair grows old.

There, active vigour never tires,
   And pleasures never pall:
No selfish aims, no vain desires,
   Where each is loved by all.

Our life is hid with Christ our Head:
   The life He lives above,
His saints shall share, when perfected,
   In glory, joy, and love.

"Come, for all things are now ready."—Luke xiv. 17.

WELCOME, welcome! Sinner, hear!
Hang not back through shame or fear.
Doubt not, nor distrust the call:
Mercy is proclaimed to all.

Welcome to the offered peace:
Welcome, prisoner, to release.
Burst thy bonds; be saved; be free
Rise and come; He calleth thee.

Welcome, weeping penitent!
Grace has made thy heart relent.
Welcome, long-estranged child!
God in Christ is reconciled.

Welcome to the cleansing fount,
Springing from the sacred mount;
Welcome to the feast divine,
Bread of life, and living wine.

All ye weary and distressed!
Welcome to relief and rest.
All is ready: hear the call;
There is ample room for all.

None can come that shall not find,
Mercy called whom grace inclined;
Nor shall any willing heart
Hear the bitter word, Depart.

Oh the virtue of that price,
That redeeming sacrifice!
Come, ye bought, but not with gold:
Welcome to the sacred fold!

"Lord, that I may receive my sight."—Luke xviii. 39.

SON OF DAVID, throned in light!
   Thou wert eyes unto the blind.
Lord! that I may have my sight!
   Heal the darkness of my mind;
That I may behold Thy face,
In the glory of Thy grace.

Give me in Thy light to see
   Things invisible to sense;
Future things as they shall be,
   Truth in all its evidence;
That my feet may keep the road
Leading to Thy high abode.

On the open volume shine,
   That I there may read aright,
All the mystery divine
   Beaming on my inmost sight;
Till Thy glory's mirrored rays
Shall transform me as I gaze.

"My sheep hear my voice .... and I give unto them eternal life; and they shall never perish."—John x. 27, 28.

THEY whom The Father giveth,
   By covenant to The Son,
Must live, because He liveth,
   And Christ and they are one.
The soul He deigns to cherish,
Can never, never perish.

Who, then, from His embraces
   Can pluck His ransomed sheep?
Earth has no hidden places;
   His eyelids never sleep:
The keys of death He beareth;
Their heaven He now prepareth.

Their sins—The Lord hath borne them;
   The Law, He satisfied:
Transgressions—yes, they mourn them,
   But, Tempter, Jesus died.
My soul thy charge denieth:
'Tis God that justifieth.

The body where His Spirit
  As in a temple dwelt,
Corruption may inherit;
  But, from its ruins built,
Shall rise—oh, far excelling!
The soul's immortal dwelling.

Christ watches o'er the embers
  Of all His faithful dead:
There's life for all the members
  In Him, the Living Head.
Their dust He weighs and measures;
Their every atom treasures.

He once, a Victor bleeding,
  Slew Death, destroyed the Grave:
Now, throned, yet interceding,
  He lives thy soul to save.
He comes—O day of wonder!
The graves are rent asunder.

But oh, that vast transition!
  How shall a creature dare
Gaze on the awful vision,
  To find a Saviour there?
Those whom He deigns to cherish,
Shall never, never perish.

His mercy shall prevent them,
　His righteousness invest :
He shall Himself present them
　Before The Father, dressed
In robes of spotless whiteness,
All beauty, joy, and brightness

"Lord! if Thou hadst been here, my brother had not died."—
John xi. 21.

O LORD! hadst Thou been here! But when
  Is not the Saviour nigh?
His power and love were present then,
  Though Lazarus needs must die.

And when the Master seems to stay,
  Regardless of our grief,
His tarrying never is delay,
  But well-timed, sure relief.

He loves to come when others flee;
  Or, coming, cannot aid;
To save in Faith's extremity,
  When hope's last glimmerings fade.

The house of mourning He prefers
  With voice of love to cheer;
And sorrows are the harbingers
  That say, The Lord is near.

Lord! not in sorrow's hour alone
  We ask to feel Thy grace:
The hearts that once Thy love have known,
  Would be Thy dwelling-place.

"That where I am, ye may be also."—John xiv. 3.

WHITHER, when I drop this clay,
    Shall my spirit wing away?
Words of life—enough for me:
" That, where I am, ye may be."

Yet, how reach that high abode?
By what long and untried road?
Hear again the Saviour say:
" Lo! I am myself the Way."

Christ the Way, and Christ the Guide,
Ill can ne'er my soul betide:
Brief the moments that suffice
For the flight to Paradise.

Absent from this mortal frame,
Yet, in consciousness, the same,
Death shall swift access afford
To the presence of The Lord.

'Twas for this the Saviour died;
That, redeemed and sanctified,
Waking, sleeping with the dead,
We might live with Christ our Head.

"Those that Thou gavest me, I have kept."—John xvii. 12.

How safe were those whom Jesus kept;
  For whom His prayer prevailed!
The Master watched while Peter slept,
  Or else his faith had failed.

Shepherd of Souls, to whom are known
  Thy chosen sheep by name!
From Satan's wiles defend Thine own,
  Nor put my hope to shame.

Let not the world's seductions win
  This faithless heart from Thee:
From lurking tendencies to sin,
  Cleanse me, and set me free.

From pride of wealth, from servile need,
  From heart-corroding cares;
From deadening heresies of creed,
  From folly's softer snares;

From sloth, excess, and avarice,
  From sordid lust of gold;
From every decent, specious vice,
  Thy servant, Lord! withhold.

Oh, by how many a fatal road
  Thy wilful sheep may stray!
Till safe within Thy blest abode,
  Be Thou, O Christ, my Way!

"No condemnation now to them which are in Christ Jesus."—
Rom. viii. 1.

No condemnation, no condemnation,
  Those who are in Christ may dread:
They have full salvation, through His expiation,
  Life in Him their living Head.
His boundless merit they by faith inherit:
  This before the throne they plead.
They in the Beloved ever stand approved:
  Christ is all His people need.

"Howbeit the Most High dwelleth not in temples made with hands."—Acts vii. 48.

[Written for the Centenary Commemoration of Whitfield's Open-air Ministry, on Stinchcombe Hill, July 30, 1839.]

How sweet, from crowded throngs,
   Zion, ascend thy songs,
With choral swell through echoing aisles!
   Where brethren brethren meet,
   Those songs rise doubly sweet,
From lowly roofs or lofty piles.

   But here, not made with hands,
   A nobler temple *stands:*
Here, mid thy *works,* O *God!* we *bow,*
   Where *all* around, above,
   Proclaims Thy power, Thy love:
Attune our hearts to praise Thee now.

   We bless Thy gracious care
   For many a house of prayer,
Where saints may meet with conscience free,
   To keep the simple rites,
   In which Thy Church delights,
And, unforbidden, wait on Thee.

But now, beneath the sky,
    We raise our songs on high,
To Him who gave all nature birth;
    While the free air wafts round
    To distant vales the sound,—
Praise to the Lord of Heaven and Earth.

    So, to the mountain air,
    The Saviour breathed His prayer:
So, 'mid green hills, or deserts rude,
    The poor He meekly taught,
    And gracious wonders wrought,
Or fed the famished multitude.

    So did Apostles teach;
    So did Reformers preach;
These hills have echoed to their prayer.
    So, let the Saving Word,
    Throughout our land be heard,
Free as the light and vital air.

"If God be for us, who can be against us?"—Rom. viii. 31—38.

If all the world abhor us,
  Or, Satan, thou arraignst us,
If God, if God be for us,
  Who then can be against us?
Its foes the soul contemneth,
  Whom God hath justified.
Who is He that condemneth,
  Since it is Christ that died?

Yea, risen and ascended,
  He now our cause is pleading:
There, till this world be ended,
  For ever interceding.
From Him, no separation
  His saints can apprehend:
He who is their salvation,
  Will save them to the end.

Not present pains or evils,
  Nor sorest tribulations,
Not tyrants, no! nor devils,
  With all their fierce temptations;
Nor aught of man's endeavour,
  Nor death, nor powers above,
The ransomed soul can sever
  From Jesus and His love.

"Rejoicing in hope; patient in tribulation."—Rom. xii. 12.

When I can trust my all with God,
   In trial's fearful hour,—
Bow, all resigned, beneath His rod,
   And bless His sparing power;
A joy springs up amid distress,—
A fountain in the wilderness.

Oh! to be brought to Jesus' feet,
   Though sorrows fix me there,
Is still a privilege: and sweet
   The energies of prayer,
Though sighs and tears its language be,
If Christ be nigh, and smile on me.

Then blessed be the hand that gave;
   Still blessed when it takes.
Blessed be He who smites to save,
   Who heals the heart He breaks.
Perfect and true are all His ways,
Whom heaven adores and death obeys.

"All things are yours."—1 Cor. iii. 21.

UPHOLDEN by the hand
  On which my faith has hold,
Kept by God's mighty power, I stand
  Secure within the fold.

Weak, fickle, apt to slide,
  His faithfulness I've proved;
Because I in The Lord confide,
  I never shall be moved.

Beset with fears and cares,
  In Him my heart is strong:
All things, in life and death, are theirs,
  Who to The Lord belong.

"Ye do show the Lord's death till He come."—1 Cor. xi. 26.

EIGHTEEN centuries have fled,
Since our Saviour broke the bread,
And this sacred feast ordained,
Ever by His Church retained.
Those His body who discern,
Thus shall meet till His return.

Through the Church's long eclipse,
When, from priest or pastor's lips,
Truth divine was never heard,—
'Mid the famine of the word,
Still these symbols witness gave
To His love who died to save.

All who bear the Saviour's name,
Here their common faith proclaim.
Though diverse in tongue or rite,
Here, one body, we unite;
Breaking thus one mystic bread,
Members of one common Head.

Come, the blessed emblems share,
Which the Saviour's death declare.
Come, on truth immortal feed!
For His flesh is meat indeed.
Saviour! witness with the sign,
That our ransomed souls are thine.

" If the dead rise not, then is not Christ raised."—1 Cor. xv. 16.

IF the dead rise not, then is Christ not raised,
   Had Christ not risen, then our faith were vain,
And all had perished. But, His name be praised,
   The saints who sleep in Christ shall rise again.

For He has risen as His people's Head,
   First-fruits of those who slumbered in the grave.
As all in Adam died, so all the dead
   Have life in Him who died and rose to save.

Not all shall sleep, but we shall all be changed;
   This mortal put on immortality:
The risen dead in glorious orders ranged,
   And death be swallowed up in victory.

The Lord with sound of trumpet will descend,
   Bringing the souls He long has kept in ward,
Now, clothed like Him, the triumph to attend:
   So shall we be for ever with The Lord.

"O Death! where is thy sting?"—1 Cor. xv. 55.

VITAL spark of heavenly flame!
   Thou must quit this mortal frame:
Yet on Christ, thy life, relying,
Death is gain: then fear not dying.
Soon shall cease this mortal strife,
And death be swallowed up of life.

Hark! a voice from heaven has said,
" Blessed are the pious dead."
Why should earth so fondly twine
Round this fainting heart of mine?
Holy Spirit! Quickening Breath!
Be Thou my spirit's life in death.

The world recedes: be gone, my fears.
Beyond the narrow stream appears
   The city of Heaven's King.
Soon shall this chorus fill the sky,
O Grave! where is thy victory?
   O Death! where is thy sting?

"My grace is sufficient for thee."—2 Cor. xii. 9.

LORD! does Thy word of promise say,
    Strength shall be equal to thy day?
Though sorely tried, I then will place
My trust in all-sufficient grace.

Weak in myself, yet, strong in Thee,
I'll joy in that infirmity
From which I learn, in trial's hour,
The virtue of my Saviour's power.

To see the burning bush endure,
May well the trembling heart assure;
Weakness sustained by might Divine,
The triumph and the glory Thine!

"One body, and one spirit."—Eph. iv. 4.

FOLLOWERS of Christ, of every name,
    To Him by faith allied;
Brethren, admit a brother's claim:
    For me, too, Jesus died.

'Tis the same human blood that warms
    Our veins, whate'er our hue;
'Tis the same blessed Spirit forms
    These rebel-hearts anew.

"Is Christ divided?" What can part
    The members from the Head?
Oh, how should those be one in heart,
    For whom one Saviour bled!

Bound to one Lord, by common vow,
    In one great enterprise;—
One faith, one hope, one centre now,
    Our common home the skies;—

Oh, let us undivided be:
    Let party-contests cease:
Nor break the Spirit's unity,
    Nor burst the bond of peace.

Then shall the wondering world again
Admire how Christians love,
And know we do not bear in vain
His name who pleads above.

"To abide in the flesh is more needful."—Phil. i. 24.

I WILL take refuge in my God,
  From man, and sin, and woe.
Fain would I drop this mortal clod,
  To know as angels know;
To love as angels love,
  And be as angels pure.
It is all light, pure light above,
  Bliss unalloyed and sure.

Yet, shall I shun the sacred fight
  Which Good maintains with Ill?
No! strong in my Redeemer's might,
  Be mine to wrestle still.
Here only, in this strife,
  Can I His soldier be;
Here only spend or lose a life
  For Him who died for me.

Nor would I too impatient pry
  The awful veil within;
Or scan the appalling mystery
  Of God-resisting sin.
No; let me be content,
  For Heaven's own light to stay.
The night, the night is well-nigh spent:
  Ere long it will be day.

"That ye may be blameless and harmless, the sons of God."—
Phil. ii. 16.

SONS OF GOD, while here below,
Let your life your title shew:
Blameless, guileless, free from stain,
'Mid associates vile or vain;
Beaming, like the stars by night,
With the Truth's reflected light:

Shewing how the doctrine reads,
Rendered into duteous deeds;
Beacons that lost wanderers bless,
Living lamps of holiness;
Shedding light on virtue's ways,
Shining to The Father's praise.

Sons of God, while here on earth,
Let your spirit shew your birth:
Let your breastplate ne'er grow dim.
Mark your Leader: follow Him.
Dread the friendship of the foe:
Spurn a portion here below.

Quench not, by an earthly course,
Life and spirit at its source:
Fear no enemy but sin;
Lose not aught that prayer may win;
Prayer, adoption's sign and pledge,
Prayer, our noblest privilege.

"Where there is neither bond nor free, but Christ is all, and in all."—Col. iii. 11.

LORD CHRIST, our glorious Head! in Thee,
No difference parts the bond and free:
The freeman owns a Master's claim;
The slave partakes a Brother's name.

From sin's eternal thraldom freed,
He that believes, is free indeed;
Free, though the limbs may wear a chain:
Tyrants would bind the soul in vain.

For those in bonds, O Lord, we plead:
Lo! Thou our Head, Thy members bleed.
To the same Body all belong:
We mourn with those who suffer wrong.

What though of different hue and race,
Brethren by blood, co-heirs of grace,
Our prayers, our sympathy they claim,
Their wrongs our sin, their bonds our shame.

Judge of the Earth, the orphan's God!
Arise and break the oppressor's rod:
Set Thou the sons of bondage free,
And all be subject, Lord, to Thee.

"I will that men pray everywhere."—1 Tim. ii. 1.

WHAT mean the sophists cold,
    Who in stern jargon hold,
That unregenerate man may not implore
    The care or gifts of Heaven,
    Nor sue to be forgiven,
Nor Nature's God, by Nature taught, adore?

    What can they mean who say,
    The sinner cannot pray,
His prayer is sin, his cry will not be heard;
    On God he may not call,
    The Father of us all;—
Thus making void the promise of His word?

    Prayer is the cry of need,
    And will not He give heed,
Who hears the ravens when they cry for food?
    Prayer is the suppliant's plea:
    How rich in mercy He
Whose sun beams on the evil and the good!

    Pray, sinner, though thy case
    Afford no sign of grace:

Pray for thy life, for pardoning mercy pray.
    Who knows but God may hear
    The cry of trembling fear,
Forgive and take the heart of stone away.

    Is want of faith thy grief?
    Pray, Help my unbelief:
Ask for the power, the heart to pray aright.
    Put forth, at His command,
    The palsied, withered hand:
Obey, thy weakness shall be turned to might.

    Then, whosoe'er thou art,
    Pray for a filial heart:
The trust that honours God, His grace rewards.
    On Him cast every care:
    Pray always, everywhere,
And let thy life's whole service be The Lord's.

"He shall ask, and He shall give him life."—1 John v. 16.

YET, canst thou pray indeed,
    And not for others plead,
Nor press thy earnest suit for those most dear?
    All prayer that can take hold
    Of promise, may be bold
In humble faith, and no denial fear.

    Wouldst thou a brother win
    From some beguiling sin?
Ask of thy God his folly to forgive.
    When faithful counsels fail,
    Thy prayer may yet avail,
And from his error he shall turn and live.

    How good to intercede
    For all, our prayers who need;
Unknown to them, to call Heaven's blessing down
    On those we fain would bless,
    Or aid in their distress,
Assured that God the prayer of faith will crown!

    How sweet, with tears and cries,
    In prayer to agonize,

Pleading for those towards whom our fond hearts
    yearn,
    And, sowing thus in tears,
    Faith silencing our fears,
Wait the sure harvest answered prayers return!

    Prayer is the censer's fire,
    Pure, warm, intense desire,
Strong will, concurrent with Almighty Love:
    For so the will of man,
    In Heaven's eternal plan,
Can move the Hand that doth all Nature move.

    Then, for this high intent,
    Brace up thy spirit's bent
To the strong purpose of availing prayer:
    Believe what God has willed,
    Shall be through prayer fulfilled:
All things are possible which faith may dare.

    And if but two or three
    Shall in their prayers agree,
Strong in the Master's Name and present power,
    The victory shall be won,
    The miracle be done,
Let them but wait The Lord's appointed hour.

"For this I besought the Lord thrice."—2 Cor. xii. 8.
"And if we know that He hear us," &c.—1 John v. 15.

YET, deem not prayer in vain,
   That does not seem to gain
Access to Heaven, though urged with tears and cries:
   'Tis thus His children learn—
   Hard lesson!—to discern,
How God, e'en then, grants more than He denies.

   He gives the strength of heart
   To bear the weight, the smart,
So wisely measured, though so keenly felt;
   The courage to resign,—
   "Father! Thy will; not mine,"—
And drink the bitter cup in wisdom dealt

   To be by Love denied,—
   'Tis then our trust is tried,
Our prayer still answered, not our fond request.
   If, taken at thy word,
   Thou hadst in *that* been heard,
Some sharper sorrow might have pierced thy breast.

   Ofttimes our answered prayers,
   Like angels, unawares

We entertain in forms of strange disguise ;
    Nor know with what intent
    Those trials have been sent,
That come on gracious errands from the skies.

    To ask is not to pray,
    But, sweetly to obey,
With filial heart, to trust, and meekly wait,
    And rest upon His will,
    Till God His word fulfil ;
For Mercy's answer never comes too late.

    If seems thy prayer in vain,
    Pray in a bolder strain,
For lofty things that best deserve thy care :
    Pray for thy country's peace,
    The Church's large increase ;
And God will hear and bless thee in thy prayer.

    If still thy flagging mind
    To prayer be disinclined,
Call up the countless mercies of thy days,
    Till thy full heart runs o'er,
    And then thy God adore,
Constrained to turn thy prayer to joyful praise.

"A vessel unto honour, sanctified, and meet for the Master's use."
2 Tim. ii. 21.

OH, how should those be clean who bear
   The vessels of The Lord!
How should those give themselves to prayer
   Who minister His word!

Cleanse me, O Lord!—my head, my feet,
   And a pure heart induce,
That I may be a vessel meet
   For Thy most holy use.

Oh, may the beamings of Thy grace,
   Reflected on my mien,
When called a sinful world to face,
   Shew where my soul has been.

Then shall I not be greatly moved
   By envy or applause,
Content to be by Thee approved,
   And glorying in Thy cause.

"I have fought a good fight: I have finished my course."
2 Tim. iv. 6—8.

WHAT joy, when life seems almost spent,
 And our departure near at hand,
To feel serenely confident
 That we in Christ accepted stand!

That life's great combat is achieved,
 That we our course assigned have run,
Have kept the faith we have received,
 And that our Master's work is done.

But, oh! for service poor as mine,
 Too high a prize the victor's crown.
The honours which Thy hands assign,
 Lord! at Thy feet I'll cast them down.

"Whither the forerunner is for us entered."—Heb. vi. 20.

FORERUNNER of His ransomed Host,
   Our Great High Priest passed through the sky,
And, on the day of Pentecost,
   Gave tokens of His power on high.

But not alone He reigneth there:
   Opening the way, He went before,
The many mansions to prepare
   For those who at His feet adore.

Where all the spirits of the just
   Worship The Lamb in sweet accord,
When absent from the flesh, we trust
   There to be present with The Lord.

"Not forsaking the assembling of ourselves together."—Heb. x. 25.

COME to the House of Prayer,
  All ye who fear The Lord,
To seek His presence there,
  To hear His holy word:
With reverence come; with sacred joy
Your voices in His praise employ.

Come to the House of Prayer,
  Ye people, great and small,
In the rich feast to share
  Which Mercy spreads for all.
Ye hungry, here is heavenly food;
Oh, taste and see The Lord is good.

Come to the House of Prayer,
  Ye burdened and distressed:
Cast on The Lord your care:
  In Christ you shall find rest.
To Heaven your hearts and voices raise,
Where all your worship shall be praise.

"Looking unto Jesus."—Heb. xii. 2.

COMRADES of the heavenly calling,
    Racers in the Christian course,
Would you keep from fault or falling,
    Proof against temptation's force,
        Look to Jesus,
Of your life the Living Source.

Mammon, Pleasure, Fame, Ambition,
    Spread their lures on every side:
Unbelief and superstition
    Would dissuade you or misguide:
        Look to Jesus;
Nor let aught your heart divide.

Look to Him who every trial
    Meekly suffered, free from sin:
Think upon His self-denial,
    When corruption stirs within:
        Look to Jesus:
Bear the Cross, the Crown to win.

He who trod the course before thee,
    High is seated at the goal.

Unseen throngs are bending o'er thee:
  See the victor's wreath and stole:
    Look to Jesus,
  And new life shall nerve thy soul.

His own hand, the Great Awarder,
  Shall His faithful servants crown.
At His feet each shining order
  Then shall cast their honours down:
    Thine, Lord Jesus,
  All the glory, praise, renown!

To the general assembly and church of the firstborn."—Heb. xii. 23.

WHAT if those registered on high,
   The loyal and the true,
The living Church, to mortal eye
   Seem scattered here and few,—
Their growing numbers fill the sky,
   Whose footsteps we pursue.

The angels who have kept their prime,
   What countless hosts are they!
The saved, the just of every time,
   Who can their numbers say?
And hour by hour, from every clime,
   They swell the bright array.

O Zion, be my name enrolled
   A citizen of thine;
Light by the things of earth I'll hold,
   Nor at their loss repine.
I soon shall tread thy streets of gold,
   And in thy glory shine.

"We have an altar, whereof they have no right to eat which serve the tabernacle."—Heb. xiii. 10.

WE have an Altar, not of stone,
   Nor reared by human hands:
Accessible to Faith alone,
   Above the heavens it stands:
Its rites require no mortal priest,
Nor Levites share our altar-feast.

The blood upon that Altar spilt
   Still and for ever pleads.
No other sacrifice for guilt
   The contrite sinner needs:
Safe when this Refuge he draws near:
Touch but the Altar, he is clear.

Yet, though with no atoning rites,
   A sacrifice we bring,—
The spirit in which God delights,
   Ourselves the offering;
And while to heaven our hearts we lift,
This Altar sanctifies the gift.

Through Him, once Victim, ever Priest,
   We have to God access:
Partakers of the heavenly feast,
   Our Saviour's name we bless:
And love and duteous deeds shall be
Our life's incessant liturgy.

"Casting all your care upon Him, for He careth for you."
1 Pet. v. 2.

When anxious thoughts the bosom fill,
  And skies look dark above,
How sweet, reposing on His will,
  To feel that God is Love!
To Him our mean affairs
  Are most minutely known:
He weighs the burden of our cares,
  And numbers every groan.

When fails each earthly confidence,
  And friends grow cool and strange,
I rest on Thine Omnipotence,
  On Love that cannot change.
This trust can ne'er delude;
  Thy goodness is most wise;
And in Thy bounteous plenitude
  My wealth, my portion lies.

Oh, let me still a Father's hand
  In all Thy ways perceive,
And, when I cannot understand,
  Be humble and believe:
Till what I know not now,
  Shall all be clearly shewn,
When at Thy throne my soul shall bow,
  And know as I am known.

"He that saith he abideth in Him ought himself also so to walk, even as He walked."—1 John ii. 6.

ART thou discipled to The Lord,
 A follower of The Lamb of God?
And dost thou hope for Heaven's reward?
 Walk in the steps He trod.

Be this thy glory, this thy shame,
 To bear His yoke the Cross who bore;
If thou dost love thy Master's name,
 Put on the garb He wore.

Art thou by His own Spirit taught,
 Let not thy lamp of life grow dim:
Be this thy very law of thought,
 To think, feel, act like Him.

Dare not what He would not have done;
 Be pure, as Christ thy Lord was pure:
Looking to Him, thy life-course run:
 Make thine election sure.

So, fashioned to a heavenly mould,
 As Grace its impress shall afford,
Thou shalt with joy His face behold,
 Transfigured like thy Lord.

"The Lamb, which is in the midst of the throne . . . shall lead them unto living fountains of waters."—Rev. vii. 17.

OH, the hour when this material
   Shall have vanished as a cloud,
When, amid the wide ethereal,
   All the invisible shall crowd;
And the naked soul, surrounded
   With realities unknown,
Triumph in the view unbounded,
   Feel herself with God alone.

In that sudden, strange transition,
   By what new and finer sense
Shall she grasp the mighty vision,
   And receive its influence?
Angels, guard the new immortal
   Through the wonder-teeming space,
To the everlasting portal,
   To the spirit's resting-place.

Will she then, with fond emotion,
   Aught of human love retain?
Or, absorbed in pure devotion,
   Will no earthly trace remain?
Can the grave those ties dissever,
   With the very heart-strings twined?

Must she part, and part for ever,
  With the friend she leaves behind?

No: the past she still remembers.
  Faith and hope, surviving too,
Ever watch those sleeping embers,
  Which must rise and live anew.
For the widowed, lonely spirit,
  Waiting to be clothed afresh,
Longs perfection to inherit,
  And to triumph in the flesh.

Angels, let the ransomed stranger
  In your tender care be blest,
Hoping, trusting, safe from danger,
  Till the trumpet end her rest;
Till the trump which shakes creation
  Through the circling heavens shall roll,
Till the day of consummation,
  Till the bridal of the soul.

Can I trust a fellow-being?
  Can I trust an angel's care?
O thou merciful All-seeing!
  Beam around my spirit there.
Jesus, blessed Mediator!
  Thou the airy path hast trod:
Thou the Judge, the Consummator!
  Shepherd of the fold of God!

Blessed fold! no foe can enter,
  And no friend departeth thence.
Jesus is their sun, their centre;
  And their shield, Omnipotence.
Blessed! for the Lamb shall feed them,
  All their tears shall wipe away,
To the living fountains lead them,
  Till fruition's perfect day.

Lo! it comes, that day of wonder!
  Louder chorals shake the skies.
Hades' gates are burst asunder:
  See! the new-clothed myriads rise!
Thought! repress thy weak endeavour:
  Here must reason prostrate fall.
Oh, the ineffable For Ever,
  And the Eternal All in All!

"And they sing the song of Moses the servant of God, and the song of the Lamb."—Rev. xv. 3.

THE followers of The Lamb who stand
On Zion's hill, a rescued band,
In grateful strains for Hell's defeat,
The hymn of Moses thus repeat:

How great the wonders, passing thought,
Lord God Almighty, Thou hast wrought!
Just are Thy ways, and sure Thy word,
Thou King of kings, earth's sovereign Lord.

Who shall not bow before Thy throne?
Thrice holy is Thy Name alone.
All nations shall their homage yield,
For now Thy judgments stand revealed.

Salvation, glory, honour, might,
To Him who reigns enthroned in light:
Worthy The Lamb, who once was slain,
Upon The Father's throne to reign.

"Alleluia! for the Lord God Omnipotent reigneth."—Rev. xix. 6.

THE Lord is King! lift up thy voice,
O earth, and all ye heavens, rejoice!
From world to world the joy shall ring:
The Lord Omnipotent is King.

The Lord is King! who then shall dare
Resist His will, distrust His care,
Or murmur at His wise decrees,
Or doubt His royal promises?

The Lord is King! Child of the dust,
The Judge of all the earth is just.
Holy and true are all His ways:
Let every creature speak His praise.

He reigns! ye saints, exalt your strains:
Your God is King, your Father reigns;
And He is at The Father's side,
The Man of love, the Crucified.

Come make your wants, your burdens known,
He will present them at the throne;
And angel-bands are waiting there,
His messages of love to bear.

Oh, when His wisdom can mistake,
His might decay, His love forsake,
Then may His children cease to sing,
The Lord Omnipotent is King.

Alike pervaded by His eye,
All parts of His dominion lie;
This world of ours and worlds unseen,
And thin the boundary between.

One Lord, one empire, all secures:
He reigns,—and life and death are yours.
Through earth and heaven one song shall ring,
The Lord Omnipotent is King.

"And I saw heaven opened, and behold a white horse, and He that sat upon him was called Faithful and True."—Rev. xix. 11.

ALREADY dawns that glorious day
  When He, the Faithful and the True,
Shall bow the nations to His sway,
  And all the Powers of Ill subdue.

No martial hosts the Conqueror leads,
  No earthly weapons win the fight:
The sword that from His mouth proceeds,
  Shall through the hearts of rebels smite.

His Word shall wither and consume
  The False Usurper in that hour;
A bright epiphany illume
  The earth, that shall destroy his power.

Bloodless the triumph of the Saints;
  Yet thrones must fall and blood shall flow,
When, to redress the earth's complaints,
  Her tyrants meet their overthrow.

And evil men, like birds of prey,
  Shall batten on the wealth and pride
Of those who held imperial sway,
  And hierarchs false, in crimson dyed.

Then shall the Church rejoice to see
   Her persecutors changed or slain :
The Dragon chained, the Slave set free,
   Justice and Truth and Peace shall reign.

This is the Age by seers foretold;
   God's will on earth shall then be done;
The Church below one sacred fold,
   All kingdoms subject to The Son.

New joy, in rapturous strains expressed,
   Through Heaven's adoring ranks shall spread;
And all the spirits of the Blessed
   Share in the triumph of their Head.

"And the Spirit and the Bride say, Come."—Rev. xxii. 17.

SEE the ransomed millions stand,
　Palms of conquest in their hand;
This before the throne their strain:
Hell is vanquished; Death is slain.
Blessing, honour, glory, might,
Are the Conqueror's native right:
Thrones and Powers before Him fall,
Lamb of God, and Lord of all.

Hasten, Lord, the promised hour!
Come, in glory and in power!
Still Thy foes are unsubdued:
Nature sighs to be renewed.
Time has nearly reached its sum,
All things, with Thy bride, say, Come
Jesus, whom all worlds adore,
Come, and reign for evermore.

"But now they desire a better country."—Heb. xi. 10.

SHEPHERD of Thine Israel! lead us,
    Pilgrims through this desert land;
Thou who hast from bondage freed us,
    Guard us by Thy mighty Hand.
        Daily feed us,
Till we reach the heavenly strand.

As Thou didst in wondrous manner
    Guide Thy chosen flock aright,
Let Thy presence be our banner,
    Cloud by day and fire by night:
        Thy protection
Be our shield, Thy word our light.

When we come to Death's dark river,
    And should we dread the swelling tide,
Death of death! Life's Source and Giver!
    Bid the narrow stream divide.
        Joyful praises
We will sing on Canaan's side.

[It is not quite certain whether the Author designed this Hymn to be included. It originated in an attempt to render a well-known imitation from the Welsh, the popularity of which far exceeds its poetical merit, more worthy of the place it has won in our psalmody. But so little is borrowed, beyond the form and leading thought, that the foregoing seems fairly to rank as an original composition.—E. R. C.]

DIVINE FOOTPRINTS.

Jehovah-jireh. Gen. xxii. 14.

WHEN thy faith is sorely tried,
   Wondering how will God provide,
On His gracious promise lean ;—
In the Mount it shall be seen.

Beth-el. Gen. xxviii. 19.

God is in the loneliest spot,
Present, though thou know it not.
Morning vows and evening prayer
Make a Beth-el everywhere.

Mahanaim. Gen. xxxii. 2.

Go where duty guides thy feet;
There good angels thou shalt meet;
Hosts of God, thou canst not see,
Watch thy steps and wait on thee.

Peni-el. Gen. xxxii. 20.

Dear and hallowed is the place
Where The Lord reveals His face :
Still He grants the blessing where
Israel prevails by prayer.

Jehovah-nissi. Exod. xvii. 15.

What if foes the Church assail?
Faith is mighty to prevail:
Pray, and Amalek shall yield;
God our Banner in the field.

Jehovah-shalom. Judges vi. 24; vii. 14.

When His saints are sore oppressed,
Gideon's sword shall give them rest:
God, who maketh wars to cease,—
God will give His people peace.

Eben-ezer. 1 Sam. vii. 14.

Safely, through another stage
Of my earthly pilgrimage,
God has helped me: to His praise,
I my Eben-ezer raise.

Jehovah-shammah. Ezek. xlviii. 35.

Zion, City of the Blessed,
Happy seat of heavenly rest!
God's abode, where is no night,—
God its glory, Christ its light.

HYMNS

BY

MRS. JOSIAH CONDER.

One mild rebuke, their terror blaming,
   Gave earnest of His power to save,
While with august command proclaiming
   His kingly rule o'er wind and wave.

The crested tides in fury seething,
   And stormy gales His word fulfil,
Above their thundering tumult breathing,
   In tones majestic, 'Peace, be still!'

The conscious deep, in adoration,
   To silence hushed its thunders proud,
Confessed the Sovereign of Creation,
   And at His feet submissive bowed.

No more, Ascended Lord, Thou sleepest!
   'Tis Faith that sleeps when fears arise:
E'en then my tossed bark Thou keepest,
   And at Thy word the tumult dies.

"If I may but touch His garment, I shall be whole."—Matt. ix. 21.

NOT Thy garment's hem alone,
   My trembling faith would hold,
Though Divine compassion shone
   Beneath its sacred fold.
Thou didst own her mute appeal
Who besought Thy power to heal.

Earthly robes which Thou didst wear
   Thy glories to enshroud,
Could remedial virtue bear
   To one amid the crowd:
More than mortal health I crave,
Now Thou art enthroned to save.

That bright raiment I would seek,
   Dyed in the atoning flood,
Which can peace and pardon speak,
   Thy vesture dipped in blood:
Here my hope its refuge holds;
Hide me in its sheltering folds.

Mediating Priest above!
   My languid spirit faints
For that suit of joy and love,
   The righteousness of saints.
Great Redeemer! clothe me in
Robes which Thou hast died to win.

"For she loved much."—Luke vii. 47.

When Mary to the Heavenly Guest
   Her duteous offering made,
And, faith's allegiance to attest,
   Her weeping homage paid;

The heavy drops, distinctly traced
   On His untended feet,
Soon every stain of toil effaced,
   And gave Him welcome meet.

She with her veil of flowing hair
   The broidered woof supplied,
And ministered with gentlest care
   The rites His host denied.

Then, on that more than regal head,
   Unseen its glory-crown,
The broken alabaster shed
   Its costly incense down.

More precious than her Indian nard,
   The homage it expressed,—
The humblest, holiest regard,
   Her contrite tears confessed.

So would I bow, ascended King!
   And thy forgiveness move;
No worthy tribute can I bring:
   Thou wilt the giver prove.

So at Thy feet my faith shall live,
   By love adoring led;
My heart its broken marble give,
   But Thou the perfume shed.

"The Lord is risen indeed."—Luke xxiv. 24.

SAD Night and blissful Morn
   Their blending wings had spread,
Like angels, o'er the Great First-born
   Uprising from the dead.

Calmed was the mortal strife;
   In vain did Hell oppose:
The Resurrection and The Life
   Bade Death's dread vault unclose.

Sad friends that waited near
   A mournful vigil kept,
Nor knew their Lord should re-appear,
   First-fruits of them that slept.

Forth to the garden's gloom
   Unseen the Conqueror passed,
Where cypress shadows of the tomb
   Were o'er His presence cast.

A sorrowing form drew nigh,
   O'erwhelmed with grief and fear;
But, not unheard, her faintest sigh
   Fell on The Master's ear.

'If thou hast borne Him hence,
  Oh, tell me where, I pray,
That I may find the place, and thence
  May take my Lord away.'

One look, one sovereign word
  Revealed Celestial Might:
With trembling joy the mourner heard,
  And faith was turned to sight.

Thus, when Thy saints endure
  The hidings of Thy face,
Thy word, O Risen Lord, makes sure
  The riches of Thy grace.

May I but hear Thy voice
  Through darkest hours of night,
That sound shall make the gloom rejoice,
  And turn its shades to light.

"And the Sabbath drew on."—Luke xxiii. 54.

THE hours of evening close:
  Its lengthened shadows, drawn
O'er scenes of earth, invite repose,
  And wait the Sabbath-dawn.
So let its calm prevail
  O'er forms of outward care;
Nor thought for "many things" assail
  The still retreat of prayer.

Our guardian Shepherd near,
  His watchful eye will keep;
And, safe from violence or fear,
  Will fold His flock to sleep.
So may a holier light
  Than earth's our spirits rouse,
And call us, strengthened by His might,
  To pay The Lord our vows.

"And all nations shall call you blessed, for ye shall be a delightsome land."—Mal. iii. 12.

LAND of the Free indeed,
   Whose wide dominions own
Subjects of every creed!
   Your Christian name is known
Where'er your martial trumpet rings:
Bid it proclaim the King of Kings.

O Land, whose wondrous reign
   Its peaceful sceptre bends
From Eastern mount and main
   To earth's remotest ends!
Unsetting suns your empire bless:
Announce the Sun of Righteousness.

His throne is on your hills:
   To Him all glory give.
His train your temple fills:
   All may draw near and live.
Then, bid the seraph-missions fly,
Touched by the living flames on high.

Your conquering standards claim
   Allegiance to your sway:
Extend it in His Name
   Whom heavenly hosts obey.
O'er earth your banner is unfurled;
Then plant the Cross throughout the world.

"And they sung as it were a new song before the throne."
Rev. xiv. 3.

WHAT blissful harmonies above
   In vocal thunders swell?
The perfecting of joy and love
   What raptured legions tell?

The glorious apostolic band,—
   Do they in triumph sing?
Do prophets from the Holy Land
   Their inspiration bring?

Or from the noble army breaks
   The deep, adoring strain,
Who won their way from fiery stakes,
   And were for conscience slain?

Is it the patriarchal race
   That breathe the sacred song?
Or to the heirs of Gospel-grace
   Do the full choirs belong?

For each, for all, the Word is found
   Almighty to atone.
All, all in shining hosts surround
   The rainbow-cinctured throne.

Peoples, and languages, and tongues
  The choral anthem raise :
To every voice and speech belongs
  The work of heavenly praise.

AGNUS DEI.

TU es Verbum Sempiternum
   Patris Unigenitus;
Deus Visus et Auditus
   Cœlis Dilectissimus.
      Tibi flecti Tu es dignus,
      Agnus Dei, omne genu.

In Te lucidè expressæ
   Patris fulgent gloriæ;
Plenum Numen possidente,
   Verbo ante secula.
      Tibi flecti Tu es dignus,
      Agnus Dei, omne genu.

Infiniti Icon vera
   Cujus ens absconditur;
Lucis splendor non creatæ,
   Dei patefactum Cor.
      Tibi flecti Tu es dignus,
      Agnus Dei, omne genu.

Tui verò alta mentem
   Angelorum superant:
Filius, O mirificandum!
   Solo Patre noscitur.
      Tibi flecti Tu es dignus,
      Agnus Dei, omne genu.

Te amantes, tamen, in quo
  Pater oblectatus est,
Te colentes gloriosi
  Tecum beatissimi.
      Tibi flecti Tu es dignus,
      Agnus Dei, omne genu.

Totos orbes per beatos
  Tu solare Centrum es.
Hoc perpetuum laudis carmen
  Cœlis Dilectissimo,—
      Tibi flecti Tu es dignus,
      Agnus Dei, omne genu.

FINIS.

"I heard a voice from heaven saying unto me, Write, Blessed are the dead which die in the Lord from henceforth: Yea, saith the Spirit, that they may rest from their labours; and their works do follow them."

Printed in the USA
CPSIA information can be obtained
at www.ICGtesting.com
LVHW052344270724
786704LV00008B/695